Supporting the Emotional Well-being of Children and Young People with Learning Disabilities

Supporting the Emotional Well-being of Children and Young People with Learning Disabilities is an essential and practical resource for helping children with severe and complex learning difficulties, their classmates, their teachers and the schools that they attend. The highly adaptable materials, activities and ideas presented in this book will be useful both in the classroom and in staff training to promote understanding of emotional well-being and mental health of all pupils who may need support.

Fox, Laverty and Chowdhury cover a range of topics that engage with the school as a whole, inclusive classrooms and the individual student. Their frameworks and practical suggestions aid teachers to support the well-being and mental health of students in a variety of ways, with material tailored for classrooms and the individual student.

Supporting the Emotional Well-being of Children and Young People with Learning Disabilities is a comprehensive resource for teachers and management in special needs schools, recognising current government policies and helping teachers to understand and appropriately engage with students as individuals and as classes.

Mark Fox is a consultant and educational and child psychologist.

Tom Laverty is a specialist trainer and consultant for complex educational needs.

Sanchita Chowdhury is a specialist educational and child psychologist.

Supporting the Emotional Well-being of Children and Young People with Learning Disabilities

A Whole School Approach

Mark Fox, Tom Laverty and Sanchita Chowdhury

LONDON AND NEW YORK

First edition published 2020
by Routledge
2 Park Square, Milton Park, Abingdon, Oxon, OX14 4RN

and by Routledge
52 Vanderbilt Avenue, New York, NY 10017

Routledge is an imprint of the Taylor & Francis Group, an informa business

© 2020 Mark Fox, Tom Laverty and Sanchita Chowdhury

The right of Mark Fox, Tom Laverty and Sanchita Chowdhury to be identified as authors of this work has been asserted by them in accordance with sections 77 and 78 of the Copyright, Designs and Patents Act 1988.

All rights reserved. No part of this book may be reprinted or reproduced or utilised in any form or by any electronic, mechanical, or other means, now known or hereafter invented, including photocopying and recording, or in any information storage or retrieval system, without permission in writing from the publishers.

Trademark notice: Product or corporate names may be trademarks or registered trademarks, and are used only for identification and explanation without intent to infringe.

British Library Cataloguing-in-Publication Data
A catalogue record for this book is available from the British Library

Library of Congress Cataloging-in-Publication Data
A catalog record has been requested for this book

ISBN: 978-0-367-32136-9 (hbk)
ISBN: 978-0-367-32137-6 (pbk)
ISBN: 978-0-429-31690-6 (ebk)

Typeset in Sabon
by Apex CoVantage, LLC

To my brother, John, and my parents, who have shown me the importance of love, friendship and attachment beyond any level of disability. (TL)

To my son, Chris – for always inspiring me to seize the day. (MF)

To my parents, my husband, Aps, and my sister, Sunny, for supporting me in all my ventures and adventures. (SC)

Contents

List of Illustrations — ix

Abbreviations — xii

Acknowledgements — xiv

About the authors — xv

Preface — xvii

Section 1: Initial engagement — 1

1.1 The background to Emotionally Able — 3

1.2 A whole school approach — 6

1.3 Working together — 12

1.4 Developing a shared understanding of emotional well-being and mental health — 15

Section 2: Developing an emotionally supportive classroom — 27

2.1 The classroom — 29

Contents

2.2	The three-step process	32
2.3	The classroom strategies	44

Section 3: Supporting an individual child — 61

3.1	Understanding an individual child	63
3.2	Understanding the extent of the emotional difficulties of an individual child	77
3.3	Developing class-based solutions using Solution Circles	87
3.4	Developing community-based solutions using the multiagency team and quality circles	94

Postscript – it takes a village to raise a child — 109

References — 115

Index — 119

Illustrations

Figures

1.4.1	Special Educational Needs in 5 to 19 Year Olds by Type of Disorder	22
1.4.2	The Incidence of Mental Health Problems	22
1.4.3	The Three Factors That Affect Emotional Well-Being	24
2.3.1	Overview of the Classroom Strategies	44
3.2.1	Rating Scale for Individual Child Profile	82

Diagrams

1.4.1	The Interlocking Factors That Affect Emotional Well-Being and Mental Health	23
2.1.1	The Three-Step Cycle for Developing an Emotionally Supportive Classroom	30
3.1.1	The Fishbone of Factors That Affect the Development of Emotional Well-Being	66
3.3.1	Working Assumptions	89

Examples

1.2.1	A Completed Road Map Planner	11
1.4.1	A Vision Statement	25
2.1.1	Green Class	31
2.2.1	Green Class – Reflective Audit of What Is Working Well	33
2.2.2	Green Class – "Dreaming and Thinking Big"	35
2.2.3	Green Class – Strategies for Change	37
2.2.4	Green Class – Evaluation Record	39
3.1.1	Musa	64
3.1.2	Musa's Perspective	64
3.1.3	Boundaries for Musa in the Classroom	74
3.1.4	"Holding" Musa in the Classroom	75

3.1.5	Containment for the Class Team	76
3.2.1	Musa – Fishbone of Individual Issues	86
3.3.1	Musa – Working Assumptions	90
3.4.1	Musa – Letter of Confirmation	97
3.4.2	Musa – Focussing on an Area and Issue	100
3.4.3	Musa – Miracle Question	101
3.4.4	Musa – Scaling	101
3.4.5	Musa – Exceptions Questions	102
3.4.6	Musa – Developing an Action Plan	103
3.4.7	Musa – How/How	104
3.4.8	Musa – Completing an Action Plan	105

Activities

1.2.1	The Road Map Planner	9
1.4.1	Developing a Vision	25
1.4.2	Developing a Vision Statement	26
2.2.1	The Reflective Audit Record	33
2.2.2	"Dreaming" and "Thinking Big"	34
2.2.3	Strategies for Change	36
2.2.4	Evaluation Record	39
2.2.5	Evaluation – Collation Record	43
3.1.1	What Would the Child Say?	64
3.1.2	Separation from Caregivers	67
3.1.3	Family Security/Relationships	68
3.1.4	Interactions	69
3.1.5	Cognitive Information	71
3.1.6	The Fishbone of Factors That Affect the Development of Emotional Well-Being	72
3.1.7	Feeling Insecure	73
3.2.1	The Individual Profile of Emotional Well-Being	81
3.2.2	The Individual Profile	86
3.4.1	What Would They Say?	99
3.4.2	A Fishbone of Factors	99

| 3.4.3 | A How/How for a Child's Emotional Well-Being | 106 |
| 3.4.4 | An Action Plan | 107 |

Tables

2.3.1	Sub-Categories of the Structure of the Day	48
2.3.2	Sub-Categories of the Organisation of the Classroom	49
2.3.3	Sub-Categories of Teaching Strategies	51
2.3.4	Sub-Categories of Shared Communication Systems	52
2.3.5	Sub-Categories of Developing Relationships	53
2.3.6	Sub-Categories of the Supportive Class Team	54
2.3.7	Sub-Categories of Feeling Safe	55
2.3.8	Sub-Categories of Feeling Loved	57
2.3.9	Sub-Categories of Feeling Confident	59

Abbreviations

ABC charts – Antecedents, Behaviour and Consequences charts

ADD – Attention deficit disorder

ADHD – Attention deficit hyperactivity disorder

ASD – Autism spectrum disorder

CAMHS – Child and Adolescent Mental Health Services

CYP – Children and young people

DfE – Department for Education

DH – Department of Health

EHC plan – Education, Health and Care plan

EWB coordinator – Emotional Well-being coordinator

ICT – Information and communication technologies

IWM – Internal working model

IQ – Intelligence Quotient

IWB – Interactive whiteboard

LSA – Learning support assistant

MDT – Multidisciplinary team

NHS – National Health Service

NICE – National Institute for Health and Care Excellence

OCD – Obsessive compulsive disorder

Ofsted – Office for Standards in Education, Children's Services and Skills

ONS – Office of National Statistics

QC – Quality Circles

Abbreviations

SATS – Standard Attainment Tests

SLT – School leadership team

SEMH needs – social, emotional and mental health needs

SEN – Special educational needs

WHO – World Health Organization

Acknowledgements

We would like to acknowledge the ongoing support to children with learning and emotional difficulties that teachers, LSAs (Learning Support Assistants) and parents give unstintingly day after day. It is their emotional strength that has inspired us to write this book

We would particularly like to thank the staff at The Brook Special Primary School and the staff at the former William C Harvey School in Haringey for sharing their wisdom and experience with us

We would also like to thank Craig Allen, whose enthusiasm and hard work initially shaped the material for the classroom strategies, and the team at Haringey Educational Psychology Service for their support and friendship

"Green" class and "Musa" as described in the book are not based on any actual class or child but are an amalgam of our many different experiences

About the authors

Mark Fox

Consultant Educational and Child Psychologist

Mark has over 40 years of experience working with parents and their children and young people with complex and multiple learning difficulties. Mark taught at a secondary and at a special school in the North of England before training as an educational psychologist. He worked in Solihull, Bromley and Essex Educational Psychology Services before taking on the role of Head of National Advisory and Assessment Services at SCOPE. Here he developed an integrated model of assessment and services for people with complex disabilities. He went on to be a senior lecturer at Essex University in conjunction with the Tavistock Clinic in London where he was also Associate Director for Research and Development. Mark then became the program director for the professional doctorate training course in educational and child psychology at the University of East London, supporting the development and supervision of trainee psychologists. Mark has worked and written with Tom for over 10 years, particularly on modules for the training materials for teachers of learners with severe, profound and complex learning difficulties (DfE, 2012).

Tom Laverty

Specialist Trainer and Consultant for Complex Educational Needs

Following completion of his psychology degree in Hertfordshire Tom worked for 3 years as a residential social worker in a respite centre for children with complex learning needs and their families. After completing a postgraduate certificate in education at University of London – Goldsmiths College he worked for 21 years in a school for children and young people with severe, and profound and multiple learning difficulties. He worked as a class teacher for 8 years before becoming primary team leader and behaviour and family support coordinator. His most recent post was Acting Deputy Head in an innovative inclusive school in North London with responsibility for pastoral support. During this time, he secured a 5-year Big Lottery Grant to develop and manage a family support project for the families of children with complex needs and challenging behaviour in North London. This involved developing and managing a team of specialist support workers, as well as offering workshop training to parents and professionals, locally and nationally. Tom has now moved into supporting and training practitioners across the country. He has a special interest in understanding and addressing the emotional needs of children and young people with complex needs.

Sanchita Chowdhury

Specialist Educational and Child Psychologist/Parenting Therapist

Sanchita currently works as a senior specialist educational psychologist for emotional well-being in a London borough as well as working independently with her own company providing consultation and training for parents. She supports children, schools and families in identifying and assessing additional needs using her specialist knowledge and skills. She also supervises trainee educational and child psychologists at the University of East London as a fieldwork tutor. Her extensive training has included teaching a wide demographic of pupils in London at the primary level followed by completion of a doctorate in educational, child and adolescent psychology at the UCL-IoE. She went on to complete a post graduate diploma in mental health and parenting at UCL, whilst practicing as a psychologist and mental health professional in Child and Adolescent Mental Health Services (CAMHS). Sanchita has a special interest in supporting parents of children presenting with behaviour difficulties, alongside working directly with children and young people with emotional difficulties.

Preface

For several years we have been developing an approach to supporting the emotional well-being of children with severe and complex learning difficulties. The focus is upon what schools and class teams can do to support the emotional well-being and to protect children and young people against any future mental health difficulties – to make them emotionally able. This material, which we call Emotionally Able, has been developed within special schools however the underlying principles would apply to children and young people with special needs in any school environment as part of individual pupil planning.

The first key principle of the Department for Education's (DfE's) advice to schools is about the central role of schools in supporting mental health and well-being for all pupils.

> Schools have a central role to play in enabling pupils to be resilient and to support good mental health and wellbeing. It is important that schools promote good mental health of all pupils.
>
> (DfE, 2018, p. 4)

Emotionally Able is a framework designed to do just that for one particular group of children – to support the emotional well-being and mental health of children with severe and complex learning disabilities.

Emotionally Able is divided into three sections:

Section 1: Initial engagement

Section 2: Developing an emotionally supportive classroom

Section 3: Supporting an individual child

Each section provides material, ideas and activities for a special school's emotional well-being (EWB) coordinator or the newly proposed mental health lead (DH and DfE, 2017 Green Paper), to use and adapt for their schools. Emotionally Able is a whole school approach to support the emotional well-being and mental health of all pupils and not simply those children whose social, emotional or mental health needs have already been identified on their Education, Health and Care (EHC) plan.

Preface

The focus is on ensuring that all children can be emotionally able even if they are learning dis-Abled.

Emotionally Able builds on the government's commitment to transform the emotional well-being and mental health of children and young people through school-based initiatives (DH and DfE, 2017 Green Paper). It supports the importance of a whole school approach as specified in the DfE's advice for schools on Mental Health and Behaviour (2018). Emotionally Able has been developed over time by practitioners working in special schools. It draws on the experiences and insights of school staff which reflect educational and psychological theories of development.

Emotionally Able ensures that the emotional well-being of children with learning disabilities or complex needs are not overlooked in this commitment to improve the emotional well-being of children in schools.

Mark Fox
Tom Laverty
Sanchita Chowdhury

Section 1
Initial engagement

1.1 The background to Emotionally Able

This book is about supporting the emotional well-being of children with severe and complex learning difficulties. "Emotionally Able" is the name that we give to the collected information in this book and this includes background information and activities that you can use to either work with your class team or, if you are the Emotional Well-being (EWB) coordinator, you can introduce to the whole school. The first section provides material for a school to become initially engaged with emotional well-being – and in particular why a whole school approach is helpful as well as the importance of working as a team. This section also focusses on the difficulties of understanding the emotional well-being and mental health needs of children with severe and complex learning disabilities.

Describing a child, or young person, as having "learning difficulties" or as being "learning disabled" has a broad range of meanings. In education the term "learning difficulties" is used to cover a wide range of pupils – from those that may have specific difficulties in learning to read to those who have a lifelong disability that affects their ability to live independently. Emotionally Able focusses on those children (and young people) whose learning difficulties are sufficiently severe or complex that they will require access to specialist provision, often in special schools. They will have life-long difficulties with cognitive learning which may also be affected by physical (e.g. cerebral palsy), sensory (e.g. visually impaired) and medical difficulties (e.g. epilepsy), and those with a diagnosed condition such as an autism spectrum disorder (ASD). The UK Health system uses the term "learning disabled" to refer to largely the same group of children (and specifically those with IQs under 70). The World Health Organization (2014) uses the term "mental retardation". In this book we describe these children as those with severe and complex learning difficulties.

In the UK these children will usually have an Education, Health and Care plan (EHC plan) which identifies their needs and specifies the provision required to meet those needs. Emotionally Able is aimed at all children with learning difficulties – not just those where social, emotional and mental health needs (SEMH) have been identified in their EHC plan.

Much of the thinking around children with severe and complex learning difficulties is around the best ways to teach them and how to manage their behaviour. What is less frequently talked about is their emotional life. In recent years the government's thinking has changed so that the importance of the role of mainstream schools in supporting the emotional well-being of all children is now recognised. However, there is often still reluctance, or uncertainty, about the best ways to support the emotional well-being of children with severe and complex learning difficulties which is often only viewed as the absence of outbursts of challenging behaviour.

School staff working with children with severe and complex difficulties are often faced with a dual challenge. Not only do the children have difficulties in learning and development some may also have significant SEMH needs. These emotional elements can be deeply ingrained, difficult to change and result in a child having great difficulty regulating their emotions and behaviour. Over the years, the understanding of children's emotions and behaviour has changed. A few decades ago any emotional outburst was usually described as challenging behaviour. Challenging behaviour was viewed as something which had been inappropriately learnt and needed to be modified or changed using rewards or reinforcements. It was seen as a skills deficit and the way the child communicated their needs (see Gardner, Graeber-Whalen, & Ford, 2001 for an overview).

Emotionally Able sees a child's challenging behaviour in terms of underlying emotional problems which can be seen as the child's reaction to being under stress. Stress as the result of anxiety and anger is a normal reaction by anyone when feeling insecure, confused, frustrated or hopeless. If this is true for a resilient and mature adult how much more prevalent is it in vulnerable children who do not feel engaged, who lack supportive relationships and ultimately don't feel positive about their world. Emotionally Able assumes that when behaviour is emotional you need to support the child's underlying emotional needs to build resilience and help them to become emotionally able.

Emotionally Able initially drew from the work of Ferre Laevers who worked with young children who had emotional, but not learning, difficulties, and his development of the Leuven Involvement Scale (Laevers, 2011). His framework was extended by working with groups of staff in special schools. The experiences of school staff were used to broaden and deepen an understanding of the emotional well-being of children with severe and complex learning difficulties.

The original "experiential" approach of Laevers and his colleagues identified two key dimensions as central – the "emotional well-being" and the "level of involvement" of the learner:

> "Well-being" indicates that the basic needs of the child are satisfied and refers to the degree to which children feel at ease, act spontaneously,

show vitality and self-confidence. "Involvement" is evident when children are concentrated and focused, interested and fascinated and when they are operating at the very limits of their capabilities.

(Laevers, 2011, p. 1)

Emotionally Able has developed these two indicators reframing Involvement as Engagement, and Well-being as Feeling Positive and added an important third area – "Relationships". This new framework provides a whole school approach for developing emotionally supportive classrooms and for supporting the emotional well-being and mental health needs of individual children under the three key headings:

Engagement: When a child is immersed in an activity which they find engaging, they can be in a state of "flow" (Laevers, 2005). They feel a positive emotional response arising from their ability to make progress or move forward with something that they see as important or meaningful.

Relationships: Good relationships depend upon the child being able to make secure attachments to adults. Secure attachments mean that the child can rely on the adults in the classroom to feel safe. These emotional relationships are both an end in themselves and the means of achieving learning and progress in the classroom.

Feeling Positive: To feel positive, the children must feel safe in school. Once they feel safe, they can begin to deal with the emotion of feeling loved. Through safety and love, confidence and resilience, they begin to emotionally develop in ways which underpin and support their well-being throughout their lives

The materials and information provided within this book have been created to break down what emotional needs can look like in children with severe and complex learning difficulties. It is our opinion that expression and then support for these needs will be similar across cultures. There will of course be differences based on the home and school environments that may change across countries. These differences could include but are not limited to differences in the following: guidance and education laws describing how children should be taught, behaviour support systems usually used by settings and schools, leadership styles of schools and language differences that have subtleties in how tone and expression is recognised and accepted. Our view is that, despite these differences, the materials within this book will be appropriate for children living across the world.

1.2 A whole school approach

A whole school approach to emotional well-being requires that the school, and the wider community of parents and professionals working within the school, share some common values and ways of doing things. It means that all parts of the school work together, and it requires the commitment of the school leadership team (SLT), governors, class teachers, LSAs and all staff, involving parents from the outset. Though Emotionally Able focusses largely on the children and young people, to become embedded and successful into the future any whole school approach must also respond to the needs of the whole community including staff, parents and families.

Emotionally Able takes a whole school approach by first reviewing how supportive and responsive the classroom environment is to the emotional needs of all the children. Schools and individual classes can then provide whole school and whole class support. Following this, individual strategies can be put in place for children whose emotional well-being remains a significant cause for concern.

The government is committed to improving the mental health support for children and young people (Parkin & Long, 2018). The DH and DfE's jointly published Green Paper (2017) *Transforming children and young people's mental health provision* sets out three key proposals to improve mental health support in schools:

- To support school to identify and train a Designated Lead for mental health
- To fund new Mental Health Support Teams linked to groups of primary and secondary schools
- To pilot a 4-week waiting time to access NHS services

Emotionally Able is designed to be used by the present EWB coordinators and the proposed new Designated Lead for mental health in special schools in conjunction with the senior leadership team. The DfE recognises that the leadership team in schools need to take a whole school approach:

> The culture, ethos and environment of the school can have a profound influence on both pupil and staff mental wellbeing. Environments that are hostile, aggressive, chaotic or unpredictable can be harmful to mental health, and can lead to stressful teaching and working conditions. Schools are in a unique position, as they are able to help prevent mental health

problems by promoting resilience as part of an integrated, whole school approach that is tailored to the needs of their pupils.

(DfE, 2018, p. 8)

Arguments for the whole school approach

School planning for a whole school approach should focus on emotional well-being as well as both teaching and learning. It should focus on the emotional well-being of the whole community, staff and parents, as well as the children and young people. However, we acknowledge that Emotionally Able focusses largely on the children and young people.

Some of the arguments for the strength of a whole school approach are set out here:

1. The government is committed to whole school approaches. The first policy objective of the Green Paper (DH & DfE, 2017) is to

    Promote good mental health and well-being amongst all CYP through whole school approaches and effective joint working.

2. The research evidence from NICE shows that in mainstream schools the social and emotional well-being for both primary and secondary pupils is supported by schools adopting a whole school approach (NICE, 2008, 2009).

3. One of the problems in improving well-being in schools is that many schools (44% of primary schools and 56% of secondary schools) do not take a whole school approach to mental health provision (Brown, 2018). There is no information on special schools.

4. Whole school programmes need to focus on positive mental health rather than on behaviour problems:

    (Effective programmes) "adopt a whole school approach, are implemented continuously for more than a year and are aimed at promoting positive mental health rather than reducing conduct problems and anti-social behaviour" (Wells, Barlow, & Stewart-Brown, 2003, p. 197).

5. The Future in Mind report highlights the role of schools in the identification of need, the location of provision and the promotion of mental health. The report identified the importance of a commitment to "encouraging schools to continue to develop whole school approaches to promoting mental health and wellbeing" (DH, 2015, p. 19).

6. A review of research for The National Children's Bureau's into what works in schools to improve mental health and well-being found that a *whole school*

Initial engagement

commitment and ethos, rather than piecemeal approaches, are key to making a difference" (Stirling & Emery, 2016, p. 1).

Weare (2015) identified several key whole school strategies that have proved to be effective in promoting emotional well-being and preventing mental health problems in schools:

1. Use a "whole school approach", which ensures that all parts of the school organisation work coherently together
2. Provide a solid base of positive universal work to promote wellbeing and help prevent problems
3. Develop a supportive school and classroom climate and ethos which builds a sense of connectedness, focus and purpose, the acceptance of emotion, respect, warm, relationships and communication and the celebration of difference
4. Start early with skills-based programmes, preventive work, the identification of difficulties and targeted interventions. Work intensively, coherently, and carry on for the long term
5. Promote staff well-being, and particularly address staff stress

(Weare, 2015, p. 4)

Emotionally Able is based on these principles that fit not only special but also mainstream schools. The first strategy addressed is ensuring that all parts of the school organisation work coherently together as a team. In their advice for schools on mental health and behaviour the DfE (2018) identified that committed senior leadership is a key structure to promote pupils' mental health. One of the key tasks for the EWB coordinator is to ensure that the school leadership team (SLT) understand and support a whole school approach to emotional well-being and mental health as they set out their vision for the school.

A road map planner

Developing a road map is helpful to show the stages required to introduce Emotionally Able and to ensure that it is being used effectively. The Road Map Planner (see Activity 1.2.1) is divided into three stages – Initial Engagement, Developing an Emotionally Supportive Classroom and Supporting an Individual Child.

Each of these stages requires training workshops with the whole staff. Schools will have different ways of organising these and the Road Map Planner can be used to begin to organise how best to implement the actions in your school. Material and activities for supporting and developing each of these stages are contained in the Emotionally Able framework. Individual schools can adapt, modify and add to these materials to ensure that the materials are used most effectively in your schools.

THE ROAD MAP PLANNER

ACTIONS TO CONSIDER:

Section 1: Initial Engagement:

Raising Interest: Presentation/Consultation by EWB Coordinator with School Leadership Team

- Clarifying outcomes, material, process, time
- Developing infrastructure: ensuring structures are in place, e.g. for Classroom Profile
- Gaining commitment: workshop – our school's vision

Section 2: Developing an Emotionally Supportive Classroom:

Introduction of the Classroom Profile: Workshops for Whole Staff

- Auditing the present situation
- Implementing strategies for change
- Evaluation and repeating the cycle
- Collating the evaluations

Section 3: Supporting an Individual Child:

Introduction of the Individual Profile: Workshops for Whole Staff

- Workshop: understanding emotional difficulties
- Understanding the extent of the emotional difficulties
- Developing class-based solutions
- Developing community-based solutions

THE ROAD MAP PLANNER

SECTION	ACTION	WHO IS INVOLVED	TIME	WHEN
Stage 1: Initial Engagement				
Stage 2: Developing the Emotionally Supportive Classroom				

(Continued)

Initial engagement

Stage 3: Supporting an Individual Child				

ACTIVITY 1.2.1 The Road Map Planner

A whole school approach

| THE ROAD MAP PLANNER ||||||
SECTION	ACTION	WHO IS INVOLVED	TIME	WHEN
Stage 1: Initial Engagement				
2.2 + 2.3	Workshop – Evaluating and repeating the cycle	Whole staff	60 mins	TBC
1.1.	Informal discussion with Mary Lee (HT)	Me (JK) +ML	60 mins	3rd May
1.1. + 1.2	Presentation to SLT	Mary Lee + JK + SLT	60 mins	17th May
1.1. + 1.2	Initial presentation to class teachers	JK	60 mins	29th May
1.3 + 1.4	Inset – EWB/Mental Health – Our Vision	Whole staff	Half Day	26th June
Stage 2: Developing the Emotionally Supportive Classroom				
2.1.	Discussion – which area to focus on: Engagement, Relationships or Feeling Positive	SLT	30 mins	12th July
2.1. + 2.2. + 2.3	Inset – Auditing the classroom and Implementing strategies for change	Whole staff	One day	18th Sept.
	Collation of evaluation and feedback to SLT	JK + SLT	30 mins	TBC
Stage 3: Supporting an Individual Child				
3.1.	Complete activities around understanding emotional well-being	Class teams	Varied	TBC
3.2.	Inset – Understanding the extent of the emotional difficulties	Whole staff	Half day	TBC
3.3.	Workshop – using Solution Circles in class teams	Whole staff /class teams	60 mins	TBC
3.4.	Workshop – using Quality Circles and Solution Focussed approaches	SLT + class teachers	Half day	TBC

EXAMPLE 1.2.1 A Completed Road Map Planner

1.3 Working together

Working in a team

In schools each individual member of staff can make a difference to the emotional well-being and mental health of children. However, staff can be much more successful if they work together as a team. There are many definitions of a team, but they essentially have the same core elements of two or more people in social interaction who have some stable, structured relationship, share common goals and perceive themselves as being in a team.

Does this apply to your class team in school? Does your team have two or more staff who have some social interaction? Is there a common culture – "the way we do things around here"? Are you trying to achieve the same or similar things – in this case trying to support the emotional well-being of the children? If you do, you have the beginnings of a team. Being part of a strong class team is an important starting point when supporting the emotional well-being of children. In all special needs classrooms, there are a range of school staff (e.g. teachers, learning support assistants [LSAs], lunchtime assistants, etc.) as well as other professionals supporting children with a variety of learning and developmental needs. The work of the class team rests primarily on the teacher as classroom lead or manager supported by the LSAs. All school staff belong to a few teams. The primary team for most staff is the class team though, you are also likely to belong to some secondary teams – for example to a Key Stage team or the SLT. For whole school change to happen, all these teams must be working together.

Continuum of teamwork

Different levels of teamwork are required to ensure children's emotional well-being is supported. For example, in sport there is a high level of teamwork in a soccer team, a medium level in a cricket team, and a low level in golf. There are some aspects of Emotionally Able that require only a low level of teamwork – for example, routine activities in the classroom and around school, labelling an area or a cupboard or toys and equipment.

However, there are other aspects of supporting the emotional well-being of children that require a very high level of teamwork: for example, supporting a child who finds it extremely stressful moving from the classroom to other parts of the school. This requires a coordinated approach from the whole class team to successfully achieve a safe, successful and orderly transition that reduces their anxiety. This involves planning with the child and between the staff, with particular attention to communication and physical proximity as the child moves around the building. The team will need to pay particular attention to when the child needs physical, visual or verbal support, time and reassurance.

Bear in mind it is often the child's uncertainty about the world that causes their anxiety and emotional over- and under-reaction. If staff in a classroom are reacting and interacting in different ways as individuals rather than taking a team approach, the child's anxiety levels will rise. Similarly, different class teams need to work together to ensure, for example, that transitions within the classroom, from room to room, or year group to year group, are not unnecessarily stressful. By ensuring behavioural and emotional consistency, the staff, working as a team, take away a major source of anxiety for the child.

Formal and informal role of the class team

The formal role of the class team is to recognise the positive interdependence of the staff – that we progress better together. A good strong team depends on individual accountability where each staff member has identified individual contributions and responsibilities. This fundamentally is built on good communication where everyone is clear about their roles and responsibilities. Team members should have interconnected roles where there is a connection between their actions and those of others. This positive interdependence is based on a recognition of the shared common goals – the emotional well-being of the children is a goal for the whole team.

A very important function filled by class and school teams has nothing to do with formally getting complex tasks done – instead it is informal, giving members of the team something in a psychological or social sense. Staff's emotional well-being is very important in creating and maintaining a whole school approach. How staff relate and work together is a good indicator of the level of support for emotional well-being and good mental health available in a school.

This informal function of a team gives each member of staff a sense of belonging, identity and self-esteem in terms of doing something worthwhile. It is psychological in terms of friendship and social support. When working with children with emotional difficulties it is also about reducing team member's insecurity, anxiety and a sense of powerlessness by being able to talk about the challenges of working with children with such complex needs.

Initial engagement

In terms of building this feeling of positive independence in the class, team leaders need to ensure the following:

- Good open communication
- A climate of trust and support
- Shared goals that are clear and accepted by the class team
- That tasks are for the whole team
- That all team members are assigned interconnected roles, i.e. staff see the connection between their own actions and those of others
- That team members are recognised for their contribution and responsibility
- Any differences between staff are accepted and worked through
- There are joint celebrations

The class and school teams also need to be open and be able to talk and reflect on how they are working as a team. Team members must feel they can request help and support from other members of the team. This should therefore be built into the processes, procedures and the Road Map. Start by focussing on what is going well as a team and how you can build on the positives – rather than catastrophising on what is not going so well.

Implementing Emotionally Able requires a whole team approach with input and commitment from the class team and other school teams. It begins with a shared understanding of what is meant by emotional well-being and the mental health of children with severe learning difficulties. This shared understanding enables the class team to have a meaningful discussion about the complex issues they face supporting emotional well-being in the classroom.

1.4 Developing a shared understanding of emotional well-being and mental health

This chapter presents some background information and views about the emotional well-being and mental health of children with severe learning difficulties. This information is presented as answers to common questions from school staff. The answers are based on government policy, research and the experience of practitioners working in this area. However, most of this policy and research is based on pupils in mainstream schools – very little has been written on children with learning difficulties. The questions and answers are designed to highlight some of the complexities when working with emotional well-being and mental health. The answers are **not** facts but simply a starting point for your discussion. The material can be used for discussions in classes or with the whole school staff. Staff can be presented with the material or asked to read the material before discussing their assumptions and the issues that arise from it. At the end of the process you will be able to write a Vision Statement for emotional well-being in your class or your school.

Question 1: Is emotional well-being the same as good mental health?

Answer: **The terms "emotional well-being" and "mental health" should be used interchangeably.**

In education the term "emotional well-being" is preferred to "mental health". This largely reflects the split there is in the provision of support between education and health (and social care). Many teachers and others in education do not like to use the term "mental health" as it is often associated with mental illness (Frederickson, Dunsmuir, & Baxter, 2009). Recently there have been various ways that the government has tried to merge these two terms. For example, Public Health England (2015) have used the term "emotional health and well-being" in their guidance.

Emotional well-being usually emphasises positive psychological concepts such as resilience and a positive self-concept. In the National Children's Bureau advice for school's emotional well-being is described as involving: "a sense of optimism, confidence, happiness, clarity, vitality, self-worth, achievement, having a meaning and purpose, engagement, having supportive and satisfying relationships with others and understanding oneself, and responding effectively to one's emotions" (Weare, 2015, p. 3).

Initial engagement

This positive definition of emotional well-being is very similar to some definitions of mental health which emphasise the positive feelings associated with the term. So, for example the National Association of Independent and non-Maintained special schools in their survey defined Mental Health as this:

> A positive sense of well-being which enables an individual to function in society and meet the demands of everyday life. People in good mental health have the ability to recover effectively from illness, change or misfortune.
>
> (NASS, 2007, p. 5)

More generally the World Health Organization defines mental health as this:

> a state of wellbeing in which every individual recognises his or her own potential, can cope with the normal stresses of life, can work productively and fruitfully, and is able to make a contribution to his or her community.
>
> (WHO, 2014)

Emotionally Able uses the term "emotional well-being" as meaning the same as good mental health. If teachers are dealing with emotional well-being, then they are dealing with good mental health.

Emotional well-being is a continuum, ranging from having positive mental health to having mental health problems. A child may change their position along this continuum at different times in their life. A child with good mental health will be in control of their emotions, be engaged with the world and have positive interactions with people around them. This state allows them to perform well at school, at home and in their social relationships.

Question 2: **Should schools focus on educational attainment rather than emotional well-being?**

Answer: **No – educational attainments and emotional well-being go together.**

Government policy places great emphasis on educational attainments. For children in mainstream schools, this is tied to teachers setting expected outcomes which are believed to improve results on SATS. For children with life-long severe learning difficulties, the aim of education is not focussed on SATS but how to improve the quality of their lives. This involves developing their knowledge and skills – but also their emotional well-being. For children with Special Educational Needs one of the four key needs potentially identified in their EHC plan is Social, Emotional and Mental Health. Therefore, the expectation is that schools should have a clear responsibility to focus on emotional well-being – especially when it is specified in a child's EHC plan.

In terms of a whole school approach, the Children Act (Her Majesty's Government, 2004) placed a duty on all maintained schools to promote the well-being of children and young people. More recently the Department for Education (DfE) in their advice for school staff stress that:

> Schools have a central role to play in enabling pupils to be resilient and to support good mental health and wellbeing. It is important that schools promote good mental health of all pupils.
>
> (DfE, 2018, p. 4)

This is reflected in the work of Ofsted who are required to consider the mental health and well-being in the schools they inspect (House of Commons Education and Health Committees, 2017).

In terms of educational attainment in the UK, research has shown that the well-being of children and young people contributes to their engagement in school and their ability to raise their educational attainment (Gutman & Vorhaus, 2012). Three of their key findings were the following:

- Children with higher levels of emotional, behavioural, social and school well-being, on average, have higher levels of academic achievement and are more engaged in school, both concurrently and in later years.
- Children with better emotional well-being make more progress in primary school and are more engaged in secondary school.
- As children move through the school system, emotional and behavioural well-being become more important in explaining school engagement, while demographic and other characteristics become less important.

(Gutman & Vorhaus, 2012, p. 3)

However, once again this research was carried out with children in mainstream schools.

Question 3: Is it easy to define mental health problems?

Answer: No, it is not easy to define mental health problems.

One way of describing mental health problems is simply the absence of emotional well-being, or good mental health. Some definitions of mental health problems relate it to difficulties being able to function in society:

> A negative sense of well-being which does not enable a child or young person to function in society and meet the demands of everyday life. CYP with mental health problems do not have the ability to recover effectively from illness, change or misfortune.
>
> (Kitchener, Jorm, & Kelly, 2010, p. 5)

There are some difficulties with this definition of mental health problems for children with severe and complex learning difficulties as they all have difficulties functioning in society and meeting the demands of everyday life. The final part of the statement is still however relevant, i.e. children who find it difficult to remain emotionally stable when coping with change and misfortune.

However, another aspect of defining mental health problem is that it presents challenges to those around the child:

> The term "mental health problems" is used to describe levels of emotional, psychological or psychiatric distress that present significant challenges for the young person, their families and those who support them. This may cover a range of problems from relatively mild emotional disorders such as anxiety (which can become very serious) and mild depression to serious psychiatric disorders (e.g. psychosis).
>
> (Kitchener, Jorm, & Kelly, 2010, p. 5)

This definition identifies the distress that the child experiences. However, the resilience of the adults around the child becomes part of defining if it is a mental health problem.

The NHS takes a broader view of mental health problems. The NHS survey of the incidence of Mental Health of Children and Young People in England 2017 (NHS Digital, 2018) divides mental health disorders into four broad types:

- Emotional disorders
- Behavioural (or conduct) disorders
- Hyperactivity disorders
- Other less common disorders (including ASD)

With this broad definition their data shows that emotional disorders are the most common of these four types, affecting 1 in 12 children aged between 5 and 19. However, these types are based on children in mainstream schools.

Other terms are also used in the UK by health services for example: mental illness, psychiatric illness, mental breakdown, nervous breakdown and mental health problems. So, it is not easy to define mental health problems and a variety of terms are used – some of them interchangeably. It may be helpful if we reduce the number of labels and simply think about children's emotional well-being and those with mental health problems. Remember – only a medical doctor can diagnose a mental health problem

Question 4: Are mental health problems all the same?

Answer: No – mental health problems are not all the same.

The most common mental health problems are emotional – anxiety and depression. Others such as schizophrenia and bipolar disorder are much less common and how, or even whether, they manifest themselves with children with severe and complex learning difficulties is not clearly understood.

Anxiety: for mainstream children, anxiety is an emotional state where they feel unsafe and are worried/frightened about a coming event. Thinking patterns include ruminative thinking and exaggeration of dangers. Children with severe and complex learning difficulties often feel unsafe and therefore anxious. How much of this is tied to these thinking patterns and how much may be connected to not being able to predict what is about to/or could happen is very unclear.

Depression: for mainstream children, depression is a feeling of worthlessness about oneself and the future. It may lead to behaviours such as feeling it is not worthwhile to get up or go out. There may be a loss of appetite and changes in sleeping patterns associated with depression. For children with severe and complex learning difficulties it is not clear how depression would manifest itself. Their dependence on adults for their independence such as eating, sleeping and dressing may mask how they feel. Their understanding of the future would also affect how they experience depression.

Psychosis and schizophrenia: it is very difficult to know if children with severe and complex learning difficulties have complex delusional thoughts and feelings of paranoia. However, we do know that they may experience tactile or visual hallucinations (which may be linked to neurological difficulties such as epilepsy).

The Department for Education's advice for schools on mental health and behaviour provides a much longer list of what may be described as mental health problems than has been discussed so far (DfE, 2018, p. 11). They use the terms "mental health problems" and "disorders" interchangeably. Their advice is aimed at clarifying what are mental health problems. Their list includes the following: developmental disorders, emotional disorders, conduct disorders, hyperkinetic disorders, attachment disorders, traumatic disorders and other mental health disorders.

Initial engagement

This list potentially identifies virtually every child with severe learning difficulties. Do they really mean this?

> *Question 5:* Do children with Development Disabilities, e.g. autism or hyperactivity, automatically have mental health problems?
>
> *Answer:* It depends who you ask!

The DfE in their advice for schools (see earlier in this section) include developmental disorders as a mental health problem – and in fact specify autism as such a disorder. It is not clear from this advice for school staff if the DfE is saying that all children with a developmental disorder such as ADD, ADHD or autism have a mental health problem. Children with autism, almost by definition, will be anxious, or children with ADD will find it difficult to settle in the classroom. However, is this more helpfully seen as part of their developmental difficulties and not as a mental health problem?

The National Autistic Society state that autism is not a mental health problem. However, they recognise that as many as 71% of children with autism have mental health problems, such as anxiety disorders, depression, and obsessive-compulsive disorder (OCD) (NAS, 2010).

This type of diagnostic overshadowing is common for children with Special Educational Needs. In the past hearing-impaired children were labelled as dumb and children with physical difficulties that affects their speech (for example cerebral palsy) were often considered as having severe learning difficulties.

Emotionally Able takes the position that a child with a developmental diagnosis should not automatically be considered to have a mental health problem. So, should children with ASD not be considered to have a mental health problem as they are often anxious? Their anxiety is part of being autistic and how well they understand and can predict events in their world and not another problem – a mental health problem. The same applies to children with ADHD and ADD. Their behaviour relates to their developmental condition not to a mental health problem. This is not to say that some children with a developmental disorder do not also have mental health difficulties, or that they are not at risk of difficulties emerging in the future if their emotional needs are not adequately supported. The problem of "Diagnostic overshadowing" occurs when we assume that the emotional difficulties of a child is part of their disability rather than a mental health problem. So, for example, we don't recognise the emotional distress of a child with ASD – we just think that it is part of their disability. However, this diagnostic overshadowing can happen the other way around too for example when we don't recognise that a child with emotional difficulties has a development disability for example Asperger's.

Question 6: **Are conduct disorders, behaviour problems or challenging behaviour mental health problems?**

Answer: **No – not inevitably.**

Once again, the DfE's advice on deciding what is a mental health problem includes "Conduct disorders, for example stealing, defiance, fire-setting, aggression and anti-social behaviour" (DfE, 2018, p. 11).

In earlier versions of this guidance they make it clear that "Behavioural difficulties do not necessarily mean that a child or young person has a possible mental health problem . . . or a special educational need (SEN)" (DfE, 2015, p. 14).

When children with learning difficulties scream, hit, bite or push they have traditionally been described as having challenging behaviour. The focus was on the child's behaviour (not their emotional needs). Strategies to change were usually derived from behavioural psychology with a focus on identifying triggers and putting consequences in place in terms of rewards – and the use of time-out.

However, the NICE Guidelines (2015) on "Challenging behaviour and learning disabilities" states that the behaviour that challenges should not be used as a mental health diagnosis. Instead it should be used to indicate that although such behaviour is a challenge to services, family members or carers, it may serve a purpose for the child with a learning disability (for example, by producing sensory stimulation, attracting attention, avoiding demands and communicating with other people).

Question 7: **Do mental health problems affect many children with severe learning difficulties?**

Answer: **12% to 33%.**

It is extremely difficult to be clear on the numbers of children with severe learning difficulties who have mental health problems. The most recent data on mental health in children (NHS statistics 2018) provide very limited data on children with SEN (see Figure 1.4.1).

The data show, for example, that approximately a quarter (26.8%) of the children who had emotional disorders also had SENs. However, it is unclear how SENs were defined with only half their sample having EHC plans – and there is no information about children with severe learning difficulties. The data shows that 42.4% of the children with SENs were identified as having behaviour problems. This

EMOTIONAL DISORDERS	BEHAVIOURAL DISORDERS	HYPERACTIVITY DISORDERS	OTHER LESS COMMON DISORDERS
26.8%	42.4%	62.9%	64.8%

Figure 1.4.1 Special Educational Needs in 5 to 19 Year Olds by Type of Disorder
(*Source*: NHS digital, 2018, p. 26)

is a much higher figure that the NICE Guidelines which gives prevalence rates for challenging behaviour as between 5 and 15% of children with a learning disability.

The most robust study in the UK remains the Office of National Statistics (ONS) surveys in 1999 and 2004 on the mental health of children aged between 5 and 16 years (Emerson & Hatton, 2007). They identified 3.5% of these children as having a learning disability. However, once again, they took a very broad definition of learning disability including the views of primary carers and teachers rather than simply children who had Statements of Educational Needs (now EHC plans).

Their research showed that children with learning disabilities are more likely than children without learning disabilities to have a mental health problem. They identified that 36% (1 in 3) of these children with a learning disability had a diagnosable mental health problem (psychiatric disorder) (see Figure 1.4.2).

However, a substantial number of these children have a developmental disorder (that is – ADHD, ASD or a conduct disorder). From their data it appears that if the children with developmental disorders are not included then only 12% of the children have

TYPES OF MENTAL HEALTH PROBLEMS	CHILDREN AND YOUNG PEOPLE	
	WITH LEARNING DISABILITIES	WITHOUT LEARNING DISABILITIES
Any emotional disorder	12%	4%
Any anxiety disorder	11%	3%
Any depressive disorder	1%	Under 1%
ADHD	8%	1%
ASD	8%	Under 1%
Conduct disorder	21%	4%

Figure 1.4.2 The Incidence of Mental Health Problems
(*Source*: Based on Emerson & Hatton, 2007, p. 11)

any emotional disorder. Therefore, in a special school for 100 children with severe and complex learning difficulties you would expect to find 12 children with emotional difficulties who do not have an additional developmental disorder. Add in the children with ASD and challenging behaviour and the number is 36%. A starting point for any school may be to examine the children's EHC plans. How many have been identified as having Social, Emotional and Mental Health needs?

Question 8: Does the child's severe learning difficulties cause them to have mental health problems?

Answer: No – it is not simply the child's severe learning difficulties that cause them to have emotional/mental health problems.

There are three types of factors that affect these children: internal (or individual) factors, interactional factors and environmental factors. These three types of factors interlock (Diagram 1.4.1 and Figure 1.4.3) together and together affect the emotional well-being of children (Emerson & Hatton, 2007).

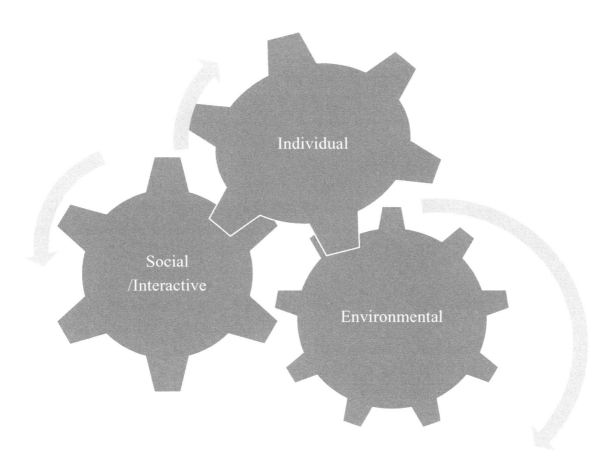

DIAGRAM 1.4.1 The Interlocking Factors That Affect Emotional Well-Being and Mental Health

Individual Factors	Interactional Factors	Environmental Factors
Physical Illness – leading to pain e.g. dental problems, constipation	Difficulties with understanding and communication	Poverty
Tiredness – lack of sleep	Poor relationships with peers	Unemployment
Anxiety – about epileptic seizures	Poor relationships with adults	Housing
Dependence – unable to feed, toilet self	Separation (hospitalisation) from parents at an early age	No garden
Physical difficulties – unable to move independently	Limited praise and social reinforcement	Two or more adverse childhood experiences
Sensory difficulties – unable to see what is around them	Parents' mental health	Lack of wider family support
Limited language – screaming best solution possible	Bullying and other forms of abuse	Lack of community support

FIGURE 1.4.3 The Three Factors That Affect Emotional Well-Being

Any one of these factors affects the other two. There is a reciprocal interaction between them – for example the individual factors affect the interactional and the interactional affect the individual.

There is also a developmental nature to mental health problems. A newborn baby does not have mental health difficulties – they do have very strong emotions. The control of these strong emotions is managed over time by the interactions they have with soothing adults. However, the adults' capacity to soothe and be available is affected by environmental factors such as poverty and housing, as well as internal factors such as the child's limited language and understanding. Mental health difficulties develop in the child from the issues that they have in all three areas – internal, interactional and environmental. The focus of this book is largely on the interactional factors. However, interventions at all three levels are helpful for the child or young person with severe learning difficulties who also has mental health problems.

Emotionally Able promotes a whole school approach to supporting the emotional well-being of children with severe and complex learning difficulties. However, government policy and research are usually focussed on children in mainstream schools. Terms such as "emotional well-being" and "mental health problems" mean different things to different people. In a special school, staff will have a wide range of experiences – both personal and professional – and consequently there is likely to be a diverse understanding of these issues. The first step in creating a whole school approach is to develop a shared understanding. Without recognising that staff start from different positions, it is difficult to implement a whole school policy about supporting emotional well-being and good mental health. Out of this discussion the class team, the SLT or the whole school can develop a Vision Statement (Example 1.4.1 and Activity 1.4.2) which underpins the development of the whole school approach to becoming Emotionally Able.

Developing a shared understanding

In teams discuss the questions below. What are your team's reflections on these questions? Write a few comments to capture your team's understanding.

QUESTIONS	COMMENTS
1. Is emotional well-being the same as good mental health?	
2. Should schools focus on educational attainment rather than emotional well-being?	
3. Is it easy to define mental health problems?	
4. Are mental health problems all the same?	
5. Do children with developmental disabilities, e.g. autism, automatically have mental health problems?	
6. Are conduct disorders, behaviour problems or challenging behaviour mental health problems?	
7. Do mental health problems affect many children with severe and complex learning difficulties?	
8. Does the child's severe and complex learning difficulties cause them to have mental health problems?	

ACTIVITY 1.4.1 Developing a Vision

OUR VISION STATEMENT

- Emotional Well-Being is at the heart of our school
- Emotional Well-Being is a goal for all our children
- All staff can make a difference to Emotional Well-Being
- We will work together for Emotional Well-Being
- No child with mental health problems will be abandoned and left behind

EXAMPLE 1.4.1 A Vision Statement

Initial engagement

Develop as a whole staff team or School Leadership Team your vision for Emotional Well-Being and Mental Health.

ACTIVITY 1.4.2 Developing a Vision Statement

Section 2
Developing an emotionally supportive classroom

2.1 The classroom

The second section of Emotionally Able focuses on the emotional well-being of all the children in the classroom. It supports the first key role of the school in the prevention of mental health problems as set out by the DfE in its advice to schools:

> Prevention: creating a safe and calm environment where mental health problems are less likely, improving the mental health and wellbeing of the whole school population, and equipping pupils to be resilient so that they can manage the normal stress of life effectively.
>
> (DfE, 2018, p. 6)

This involves the whole school staff working in their primary class teams. The aim is to identify strategies that class teams can introduce into their own classroom that will support the emotional well-being of all the children across the school. These classroom strategies are focussed on the three key areas of emotional well-being:

- Engagement
- Relationships
- Feeling positive

The school's EWB coordinator or mental health lead can provide training and workshops for the whole staff to introduce this process and to ensure that class teams are implementing the strategies and evaluating their impact.

Emotionally Able provides a three-step cyclical process for developing these emotionally supportive classrooms across the school:

Step 1: Auditing the present situation

Step 2: Implementing strategies for change

Step 3: Evaluation and repeating the cycle

An emotionally supportive classroom

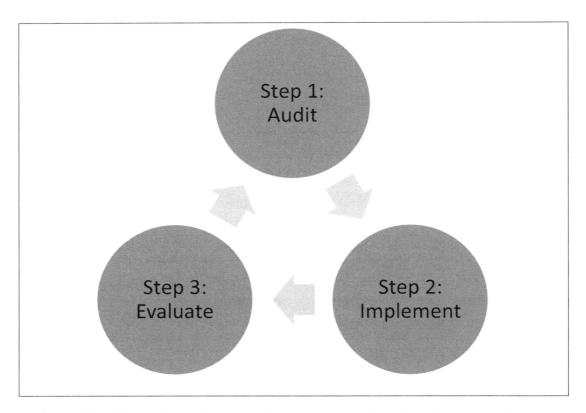

DIAGRAM 2.1.1 The Three-Step Cycle for Developing an Emotionally Supportive Classroom

As outlined in Section 1, these steps are best introduced as a whole school process. However, schools are busy places and it may not be possible to gain the commitment to introduce Emotionally Able to the whole school at the same time. If this is the case it is possible to introduce the three-step process incrementally. It may be that the three steps are initially used by an innovative teacher or are used as pilot to try out the benefits of this approach before its introduction to the whole school. However, in whatever way it is introduced, you can follow the same three-step process.

The best time to start the process, with the initial reflective audit, is at the beginning of the school year. Step 2 – implementing strategies for change – can be completed at the end of the first Autumn half-term and implemented during the second half of the term. Step 3 – evaluation – can then take place at the end of the Autumn term. This cycle can be repeated each term throughout the school year. However, you could start the process at the beginning of the Spring or Summer term and still follow the same three-step process.

Everyone in the class team should be involved in all three steps, with the strategies decided upon and implemented by the whole class team. The class team should retain the "experiential" approach of Laever and his colleagues whereby it is their classroom experience that informs the strategies you use. The strategies we have provided are based on the experiences of educational staff working daily with children with severe and complex learning difficulties. Your staff will have had similar, but also different experiences, and have developed their own ways of supporting the emotional well-being of children. Use these experiences and build them into the strategies outlined in this book. In addition, the context you are in will influence the strategies you will find successful. For example, are you in an isolated classroom with an LSA to support you or an open plan area with six LSAs moving between different areas? These contextual factors will also make a difference to what strategies you can implement.

Whatever your situation, to implement this approach, the members of the class team must all work together. You need to support the formal aspect of this with an agreement of the strategies you are going to use and to identify areas for further development. But just as important are the informal aspects of the team in terms of working together to celebrate the successes and supporting each other emotionally when things are difficult.

> *Green is a class of eight children aged between 9 and 11 in a special school. All the children have severe learning difficulties and two have complex needs – one of whom is a wheelchair user. Two of the children have a diagnosis of autism. Three of the children have very limited or no speech. The class team consists of me, Sasha, the teacher and two LSAs. One of the LSAs, June, is very experienced and the other, Philip, has just started.*
>
> *The classroom is quite large and there are two "quiet" rooms leading off from it. One is used for storage (by other parts of the school). The toilets are down the corridor. The children have their lunch in the hall. The classroom looks out onto the playground.*
>
> *Most days I feel overwhelmed by the complexity of the children's learning difficulties, their emotional outbursts and the never-ending demands of parents, professionals and the SLT.*

EXAMPLE 2.1.1 Green Class

2.2 The three-step process

Step 1: auditing the present situation

The first step is for your class team to audit the present situation in the classroom. This is a reflective audit rather than one that relies on you collecting data – for example, what are the attendance figures for each child. Instead, a reflective audit is one where you, as a team, remind each other of key incidents that have happened over the last term. This reflective audit should focus on what has been working well – ignore for the moment all the things that did not go so well. It is only too easy for people to remember all the difficult times – that is part of the problem when trying to build up positive strategies. Instead think about incidents where the children surprised you, for example with what they could do, or how quickly they became calm, or their positive relationship with each other or an adult. These are the little things, the day-to-day things that can easily become forgotten in a busy classroom. You may already keep a diary, or there may be some other record of the term – for example, photographs. It may be very helpful to use these to remind yourself of the successes you have had.

Emotionally Able is structured around the three areas of Engagement, Relationships and Feeling Positive. "The classroom strategies" (Chapter 2.3) is built around this framework and provides 9 categories and 27 sub-categories of strategies that have been used successfully. You should familiarise yourself with this material before you proceed with the reflective audit. It will help remind you of the strategies that you already have successfully in place and also help to widen your discussion. You may find it helpful to focus your discussion on only one of the key areas: Engagement, Relationships or Feeling Positive.

Some of the questions you can reflect on as a team are these:

- What is working well?
- What were the high points within this area?
- What strategies/approaches were successful/useful?
- What are the core factors in this area that make our classroom function at its best?
- What changes have there been in children's responses to you?
- What do you value most about your work as part of the class team?

What is important here is focussing upon what has been successful for both children and staff in this particular area. The challenges of what to do differently will come soon enough! Record the outcome of your discussion on the Reflective Audit Record (Activity 2.2.1 and Example 2.2.1). It is easy to forget what is going well, and this record is useful in reminding the team about the successes you have had over the term.

Name of Class:	Date of Audit:

Area: Engagement/Relationships/Feeling Positive *(please circle appropriate area)*

What is working well?

What were the high points within this area?

What strategies/approaches were successful/useful?

What are the core factors in this area that make our classroom function at its best?

What changes have there been in children's responses to you?

What do you value most about your work as part of the class team?

ACTIVITY 2.2.1 The Reflective Audit Record

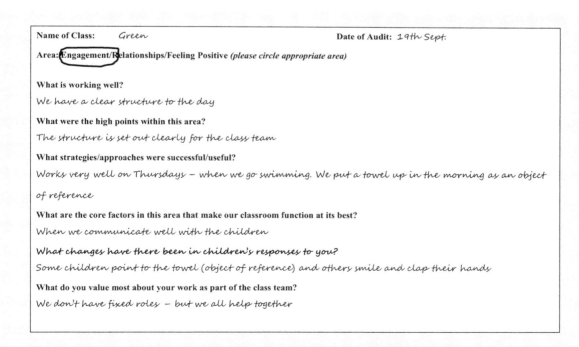

EXAMPLE 2.2.1 Green Class – Reflective Audit of What Is Working Well

An emotionally supportive classroom

Step 2: Implementing strategies for change

When the reflective classroom audit, step 1, is complete the class team can turn their attention to answering the key question in step 2: "What can be done differently?" The team should stay with the key area that they have identified in step 1 and then choose one of the three categories in the key area. They can then, as a team, identify which of the three sub-categories within their chosen category they would like to focus on in order to strengthen the support for emotional well-being in their classroom. The discussion should build upon the core factors and positive success identified in the reflective classroom audit with team members "dreaming" or "thinking big" (Activity 2.2.2 and Example 2.2.2) about what can be achieved based upon their experience and in the agreed time frame.

"The classroom strategies" (see Chapter 2.3) lists a wide variety of suggestions. These are framed as strategies and ideas that staff teams may want to consider or draw their ideas from. They are not presented as a comprehensive list but rather as a rich bank of suggestions based on the experiences of teachers, support staff and children in special schools. They provide strategies to help the class team address the needs of children with emotional and mental health difficulties within their normal teaching practice. These strategies are designed to help the whole class group with their emotional well-being and mental health.

> **Imagine it is a year from now and the classroom is just as you want it to be...**
> - What's happening that makes it vibrant and successful?
> - What has changed?
> - What has stayed the same?
> - What have you done to contribute to this future?
>
> Then:
>
> What can you continue doing to keep the "good" bits?
> What can you begin to do to make it better?
> What can you stop doing because it no longer serves or gets in the way

Activity 2.2.2 "Dreaming" and "Thinking Big"

> **Imagine it is a year from now and Green is just as we want it to be..........**
> - What's happening that makes it vibrant and successful?
>   *The children are laughing and enjoying the activities*
> - What has changed?
>   *They are no longer running off and getting upset when they transition. There is no longer any screaming*
> - What has stayed the same?
>   *We have the same team in place*
> - What have you done to contribute to this future?
>   *We have changed the activities that we offer to them.*
>   *We communicate changes more clearly to introduce transitions*
>   *We give them more choice of activities*
>
> Then – what can you continue doing to keep the "good" bits?
> *Keep the structure*
>
> What can you begin to do to make it better?
> *Develop more objects of reference so they know which day it is and which activities are happening*
>
> What can you stop doing because it no longer serves or gets in the way
> *Stop insisting on activities that do not engage them*

Example 2.2.2 Green Class – "Dreaming and Thinking Big"

At this point, ideas for the "Strategy for Change" should combine ideas from the "Dreaming and Thinking Big" with positive aspects from the previous section "What is working well". In this way the new strategies for working are drawing on a current positive and successful base.

The team should complete the "Implementing Strategies for Change" (Activity 2.2.3 and Example 2.2.3) to ensure that they have a record of what has been agreed.

In Example 2.2.3, Green class have detailed several strategies that they are going to put into place. Each of these strategies requires a commitment of time and resources. When you start to use Emotionally Able, we suggest that you initially focus on only one strategy. There is always a gap between deciding to act and acting. The smaller you can make this gap the more likely you will actually change your classroom practice. This is not to say that generating a range of strategies is not in itself an empowering and positive experience with team members, maybe for the first time, seeing how they can impact on the children's emotional well-being. Focussing on one of these, or at least prioritising these strategies, helps to make the commitment to action.

An emotionally supportive classroom

STRATEGIES FOR CHANGE		
Name of Class:		**Date of Audit:**
Area: Engagement/Relationships/Feeling Positive *(please circle appropriate area)*		
Category:		**Sub-Category:**
What can be done differently? *(Ideas can be found in Classroom Strategies)*		
SELECTED STRATEGIES	**BY WHOM?**	**START DATE**

ACTIVITY 2.2.3 Strategies for Change

STRATEGIES FOR CHANGE

Name of Class: *Green*   Date of Audit: *19th September*

Area: **(Engagement)**/Relationships/Feeling Positive *(please circle appropriate area)*

Category: *The Structure of the Day*   Sub-Category: *Structuring the day*

What can be done differently? *(Ideas can be found in Classroom Strategies)*

Selected Strategies	By Whom?	Start Date
Starting the Day Start the day with the same welcome song. Then follow up with a different action song for each day of the week depending on the activity of the day e.g. cooking, swimming, music – using an object of reference representing that activity. Repeat this for each activity throughout the day	Sasha	Now!
Transitions out of class Introduce by getting the children to touch the object of reference prior to leaving the room. Let Abbie in the wheelchair go first and talk about what is happening to give a narrative about why the class are leaving. Philip moves through the door first and stands to one side with Abbie blocking any opportunity to run leaving only the direction of the group as the available direction of travel. At the same time June or Sasha should lead the way for the rest of the group whilst one or other should be in the classroom talking to the last few in the group telling them what they are going to do. Philip should then move to the front to lead the way with Abbie ensuring that the group do not move too fast along the corridor. June or Sasha can move to the back and stay slightly behind to prevent any movement in the wrong direction. All should talk to the children as they move – offering praise and keeping the process calm and low key.	Philip, June and Sasha	Now
Flexibility in Activities Philip and June to introduce new activities during free play – playing with them themselves and making them interesting for the children. Look for interest/reactions and then build these activities into teaching sessions. Give children individual choice from a range of learning activities	Philip and June	25th September

Example 2.2.3 Green Class – Strategies for Change

Step 3: evaluation and repeating the cycle

Once you have initiated the strategy for change, you have to decide how long you are going to implement it before you evaluate its effectiveness. Sometimes these time frames are set by the school calendar, for example at the end of the half term. Sometimes strategies take longer to have an impact – especially if it is a strategy that does not happen daily but maybe fortnightly, for example a strategy about the children going to a local park. In this case you may need to leave a longer time between the initiation of the change and the evaluation. It is also important to remember that any change for many of these children with severe and complex learning difficulties can be stressful and disorientating. So initially after the introduction of a new strategy you may find the children emotionally unsettled until they understand and are familiar with the new procedures. This is not to argue against the importance of change but simply to recognise that no one likes change being done to them.

The impact of the strategies should be evaluated in terms of what difference they have made to the children's emotional well-being across the class group. Through ongoing observation and recording systems, e.g. incidental observation, class teams can establish the quality and range of improvement achieved by the strategies they have implemented in relation to the one or more chosen sub-categories. This information can be captured on the Evaluation Record (see Activity and Example 2.2.4.).

The first question on the Evaluation Record focusses on how embedded the strategy is in the classroom. This question allows the team to reflect on how much this strategy has become part of the classroom culture (the way we do things around here) or whether it is still a bolt-on that has never really gained a place in the classroom. By reflecting on this the team can become aware of how difficult it is for them to implement certain strategies and what kind of support might be helpful in the future.

The second question remains focussed on the same sub-category and asks the team how they could continue to build on the "success" of the initial strategy. We have found that swapping from category to category can dissipate the energy in a class team and make them lose focus.

The third question addresses the fact that even though the strategies focus on only one category in one area they may well have an impact in another area. So for example, though the focus may be on the area of Engagement and the class team might be looking at the children showing more interest in a greater range of toys and equipment and becoming more engaged during structured curriculum activities, they may actually find that the children are communicating more, have a greater "vocabulary" (words, sounds or signs) and are more interactive with other children and/or staff. It is therefore important to reflect on whether there have been changes in other areas of emotional well-being not simply the subcategory that was initially chosen.

EVALUATION RECORD

Name of Class: Date of Evaluation:

Area: Engagement/Relationships/Feeling Positive *(please circle appropriate area)*
Category: Sub-Category:

1. What strategy has been most successful in developing this sub-category?						
2. How embedded is this strategy in classroom practice? *(please circle appropriate area)*						
5	4	3	2	1	0	
Fully embedded	Continuing to embed	Daily practice of strategy	Building skills to address issues	Awareness of needs	No awareness	
3. How could this sub-category be further developed?						
4. What differences, if any, did the new strategies make in any other categories/sub-categories?						
(NB. You may find your answer to this question helps identify another category/sub-category to work on)						

If moving to a different area/category/sub-category go to Step 1
If continuing to work on this subcategory go to Step 2

Activity 2.2.4 Evaluation Record

EVALUATION RECORD

Name of Class: *Green* Date of Evaluation: *14th December*

Area: (Engagement)/Relationships/Feeling Positive *(please circle appropriate area)*
Category: *The Structure of the Day* Sub-Category: *Structuring the Day*

1. What strategy has been most successful in developing this sub-category?					
The different songs each morning to identify the day's activities					
2. How embedded is this strategy in classroom practice? *(please circle appropriate area)*					
5	4	3	2	1	0
Fully embedded X	Continuing to embed	Daily practice of strategy	Building skills to address issues	Awareness of needs	No awareness
3. How could this sub-category be further developed?					
Extend the use of action songs and objects of reference throughout the day					
4. What differences, if any, did the new strategies make in any other categories/sub-categories?					
Children are calmer as we continue to deal with the issues of beginnings, endings and transitions					

If moving to a different area/category/sub-category go to Step 1
If continuing to work on this subcategory go to Step 2

Example 2.2.4 Green Class – Evaluation Record

Repeating the cycle

The Evaluation Record has two purposes. It helps inform class teams of the effect of the strategy and helps to identify the next sub-categories to focus on in order to build upon their success. It also can become a means by which good practice is disseminated throughout the school (see the next section).

In terms of identifying the next subcategory to focus on a whole school approach may be used. The feedback on the evaluation forms is part of the information that the EWB coordinator can use for deciding on what should be a future priority area. The EWB coordinator may want all classes to focus on one key area, or on one particular category, that has been identified as a priority by the SLT. In these circumstances the coordinator can give a short presentation introducing the area of focus for the term ahead and why the key area, categories and sub-categories in this area were chosen. The class team will then once again complete steps 1 and 2. This begins with a discussion about what is working well in the chosen area, then "dreaming big" before identifying the strategies for the chosen period ahead. If this is a whole school approach, then the EWB coordinator can set the date for completion and submission of the strategies. They also have a role, if necessary, of offering support to class teams in identifying and setting suitable strategies.

Once Emotionally Able has been introduced to the whole school, it will be more effective if class teams individually decide on what is their next priority area to tackle. This allows class teams to decide what their priorities are – given their staff, the children and the context in which they are working. As class teams move forward in developing their understanding and a more emotionally supportive classroom environment, the process may begin to identify individual children for whom the class-centred approach is not meeting their needs. In these circumstances, the individual child-centred approach can be introduced.

Collating the evaluations

The aim of this process is to share the collated information from the evaluations. This can be done termly or yearly and identifies the success of the chosen strategies. Over time, the collated evaluations will begin to highlight the strategies that are successful in your school in the three Key Areas – Engagement, Feeling Positive and Relationships. This helps ensure a structured whole school approach to supporting emotional well-being and mental health.

Copies of the completed evaluation forms should be sent to the EWB coordinator. These can then be collated on the Evaluation – Collation Form which provides an overview of the following:

- The key areas/categories/sub-categories chosen
- The overall rate of success of the chosen strategies
- How difficult it has been to embed the strategies into everyday practice
- Any additional factors that added to the success of the strategies

This information should then be fed back to the whole school. This is best done as part of a training session so that school staff can also share their experience of the implementation of the strategies. This should include the successes and challenges as well as advice on lessons learned.

An emotionally supportive classroom

Evaluation – Collation Record

AREA	TOTAL	CATEGORY	TOTAL	SUB-CATEGORY	TOTAL	SUCCESSFUL STRATEGIES	HOW EMBEDDED
Engagement		The Structure of the Day		Structuring the Day			
				Grouping the Children			
				Timetabling			
		The Organisation of the Classroom		Organising the Classroom Space			
				Organising Resources			
				Children's Needs and Resources			
		Teaching Strategies		The Curriculum			
				Active and Interactive Teaching and Learning			
				Multi-sensory			
Relationships		Shared Communication Systems		Demonstrating unconditional positive regard			
				Using Intensive Interaction			
				Augmentative and Alternative Communication			
		Developing Relationships		Building a working Alliance			
				Building a relationship			
				Building a relationship with peers			
		The Supportive Class Team		Cooperation and communication			
				Organisation of roles			
				Knowing the children			

Feeling Positive	Feeling Safe	A Safe Classroom		
		A Safe Group		
		Transitions in School		
	Feeling Loved	Feeling Loved by the Adults		
		Feeling Loved by Peers		
		Feeling Loved by the Larger Family		
	Feeling Confident	Making Choices		
		Developing Internal Motivation		
		Becoming Independent		

Activity 2.2.5 Evaluation – Collation Record

2.3 The classroom strategies

An overview of the classroom strategies

The strategies for classroom change are drawn from the experiences of school staff working with children with severe and complex learning difficulties. The successful strategies have been shared between class teams and then further developed and modified. They are divided into the three key areas: Engagement, Relationships and Feeling Positive. Each of these three areas are then divided into three categories, each with three sub-categories, giving nine sub-categories under each of the three areas. This overall framework for classroom strategies consists of 27 sub-categories in total that staff can use. These strategies can then be adapted and developed to ensure they meet the needs of individual class teams based upon their reflective classroom audit.

AREA	ENGAGEMENT	RELATIONSHIPS	FEELING POSITIVE
Category	The Structure of the Day	Shared Communication Systems	Feeling Safe
Sub-category	• *Structuring the day* • *Grouping the children* • *Timetabling*	• *Demonstrating unconditional positive regard* • *Using Intensive Interaction* • *Augmentative and Alternative Communication*	• *A safe classroom* • *A safe group* • *Transitions in school*
	The Organisation of the Classroom	Developing Relationships	Feeling Loved
	• *Organising the Classroom Space* • *Organising Resources* • *Children's Needs and Resources*	• *Building a working Alliance between the children and the class team* • *Building a relationship between the children and the class team* • *Building a relationship with peers*	• *Feeling loved by the adults* • *Feeling loved by peers* • *Feeling loved by the larger family*
	Teaching Strategies	The Supportive Class Team	Feeling Confident
	• *The Curriculum* • *Active and Interactive Teaching and Learning* • *Multi-sensory*	• *Cooperation and communication* • *Organisation of roles* • *Knowing the children*	• *Making choices* • *Developing internal motivation* • *Becoming independent*

FIGURE 2.3.1 Overview of the Classroom Strategies

Engagement

When children are immersed in an activity which they find engaging they can be described as in a state of "flow" (Laevers, 2005). They feel a positive emotional response arising from their ability to make progress or move forward with something that they see as important or meaningful.

A.1. The Structure of the Day

To support children's emotional well-being, the school day needs to be consistent and predictable. Children need to understand what is happening and be able to predict what is happening next. This will in turn reduce their levels of stress and anxiety

A.2. The Organisation of the Classroom

To support children's emotional well-being the classroom needs to be organised in a consistent and predictable way. Uncertainty causes many children to feel anxious. It is important therefore that they recognise and become familiar with the space and activities they are involved with.

A.3. Teaching Strategies

Children's emotional engagement in learning depends on what is being taught (the curriculum) as well as how it is being taught.

Relationships

Good relationships depend upon the child being able to make secure attachments to adults. Secure attachments mean the child can rely on the adults in the classroom to feel safe. These emotional relationships are both an end in themselves and the means of achieving learning and progress in the classroom.

B.1. Shared Communication Systems

Relationships depend upon communication but building a relationship with a child with learning difficulties means more than simply speaking to them. Building a relationship depends on the attitudes of the adults, developing an attuned connection and the effective use of specialised communication systems.

B.2. Developing Relationships

Children need to build good relationships with adults and other children in school. These relationships take time to develop especially for children with emotional difficulties who are feeling insecure. The first step in building a relationship is building an alliance where the child understands that the class team is there for them. Only when they feel secure will they build relationships with the class team and peers.

B.3 The Supportive Class Team

In most classrooms in Special Schools, there is a small class team consisting of teachers and Learning Support Assistants (LSAs). This small class team is extended by several other professionals who are directly involved with the children on a regular basis. These include physiotherapists, speech and language therapists, occupational therapists, volunteers and students on placement. The strength of these people working together as a team supports the emotional well-being in the classroom.

Feeling positive

To feel positive, the children must feel safe in school. Once they feel safe, they can begin to deal with the emotion of feeling loved. Through safety and love, confidence and resilience, they begin to emotionally develop in ways which underpin and supports their well-being throughout their lives.

C.1. Feeling Safe

Adults can often pre-empt emotional distress by ensuring that children feel safe. Children need to feel that the class team can contain their emotions and help them de-escalate feelings of anxiety, fear or anger if they feel emotionally unsafe. This distress can often come when children do not know, or understand, what is expected of them, or when they are uncertain or afraid of the reactions of their peers. The uncertainty may become all pervasive at times of transitions.

C.2. Feeling loved

There are different types of love that children crave for. Three of these types of love are identified in this section. There is family love which parents, and the wider family, naturally feel for their children. It is what initially makes the child feel secure and safe and is based on forgiveness and acceptance. This is different from the class team's love which is based on altruism in terms of goodwill and an unselfish concern for the well-being of the children. Altruism is a sign of cooperative intention by the class team to help the children. Finally, there is the friendships and good will that children need from their peers. Children with severe and complex learning difficulties require all three of these types of love. They can only love and feel for others if they also love themselves.

C.3. Feeling confident

Children become more confident as they develop control over their lives. Building confidence is like any other skill – it needs to be taught. Confidence increases as the children become more independent and are able to make choices about what they do – and what they don't want to do. External rewards can be used to boost confidence – but the really confident child will be motivated to complete activities because they enjoy them.

STRUCTURING THE DAY	GROUPING THE CHILDREN	TIMETABLES
The school day should be structured into sessions, so the children understand what is happening and predict what is happening next. Repetition offers a secure foundation for children who are emotionally vulnerable. Repetition is a safe place to be. A key skill of teachers is knowing how much consistency and repetition of activity is good for any individual child both in terms of learning and emotional well-being, without reducing the child's motivation towards undertaking the activity. **Consider how you structure the day:** - Meet the child at the door - Start the day with a welcome song/game as a whole class - Use music/singing throughout the day to signal the beginning and end of activities - Consider academic activities being taught during the morning, if children are more alert at start of the day. - Use free play daily to support children in exploring/extending activities that they like. - Use lots of movement breaks at the end of sessions. - Build movement into each session. - Allow children time for their own choices and interests **Consider how you structure the sessions:** Sessions should be structured into short and simple activities that are engaging and enjoyable. Pay close attention to beginnings endings and transitions. These activities should be appropriate to the needs of the children. - Set expectations before the start of the activity. - Prepare children for each part of the activity using photographs or interactive whiteboard (IWB) - Encourage children to communicate when they have completed the activity - Monitor the levels of engagement with each activity to understand when to move on. - Allow children who show an interest in an activity to continue with it. Activities for individual children can be flexible to take into account: - Sensory needs - Communication needs - Child's own interests - Relationships	Children need to be grouped in different ways throughout the school day from individual work stations to whole class activities. This organisation will depend on the session, the activity and the differentiated learning objectives for each child. In terms of emotional well-being it is also important to consider particular friendships and the development of relationships. **Build into the teaching week:** - Whole class circle time at the beginning of the day, before lunch at the beginning of the afternoon and at the end of the day - Whole class activities - Needs led groups according to area of learning, activity and/or interest - Differentiation within the class group according to skills and abilities - 1:1 teaching for individual targets - Individual distraction free learning stations	There should be a range of timetables for different purposes in the classroom. These should reflect a clearly organised school day and school week for members of staff and children. Consistency and stability help children with their emotional well-being. **Suggested Timetables:** - Whole week timetable on information board or door for staff including staff availability. - Consistent sessions and snack/lunch schedules for staff and children - Daily visual class timetable giving clear structure to the day. - Use "now, next" symbols and objects of reference - Use of individualised visual timetable outlining the day for identified children. - Use of visual timetables to manage the access to resources. - Ensure time out of class for a child's identified need which is displayed in individualised timetable (including movement breaks, physiotherapy, manual handling, feeding) - Display for staff a list of small jobs that need to be done (e.g. batteries in toys, setting up activities) Acknowledge daily changes and differences in timetable and keep staff and children informed.

TABLE 2.3.1 Sub-Categories of The Structure of the Day

ORGANISING THE CLASSROOM SPACE	ORGANISING RESOURCES	CHILDREN'S NEEDS AND PREFERENCES
The classrooms space can be organised in several ways depending on the needs of the children and the size and layout of the classroom. It is helpful to include space for key specialised areas, for individual work stations, for small groups and whole group teaching. The floor space can be set up with different activities to offer more choices. Consider the use of the following: • The carpeted and non-carpeted areas. • The "outdoor space" (including messy play) • Identified areas for sensory sessions e.g. sand, water, sound and light • Identified areas for ICT and books	The accessing of resources requires considerable organisation. Some of the children have a great deal of their own equipment. This may include large equipment such as wheelchairs, walkers and standing frames as well as smaller equipment, for example eating utensils. As well as this personal equipment there are also classroom resources used for various activities. Ensuring that these resources are accessed and built into the timetable is of real benefit to the children's emotional well-being Consider how to do the following: • Ensure that children know about the wide range of interesting equipment in the classroom • Ensure children can ask for what they want when it is choosing time • Offer activities and resources they like and are stimulated/motivated by • Use the resources children like from the classroom and rotate and use in different ways to keep children interest • Watch the children to see what they like to do • Make use of personal boxes where appropriate Access to resources depends upon effective use of cupboard space to ensure the following: • Easy access for staff and children as appropriate to need. • Easy access to stock • Dangerous and/or distracting resources are securely stored away	Children will have wide range of needs in addition to their diagnosis. Understanding these individual needs or preferences help support their emotional well-being. Children's prefer certain activities, or being grouped with particular children, or playing with a particular "favourite" toys/objects. Children also will feel more emotionally comfortable at certain times and in particular areas of the classroom. Consider how much control children have over these preferences – who they are with, what they do and where they spend their time. Consider whether children's: • Favourite toy/objects are beside them during activities to assist them to engage. (As long as it doesn't cause problems and interfere with the learning.) • Favourite toys/objects are consistently available for "choosing time" • Favourite toys/objects are out to allow the children to play during quiet moments or to defuse anxious situations • Favourite snack time equipment/colours, e.g. "the blue plate" is used • Preference for particular areas in the classroom is recognised and met where possible • Preference for particular sequences are recognised e.g. who goes first/last • Preference for particular furniture is recognised and met where possible e.g. provision of soft chairs or sofa

Table 2.3.2 Sub-Categories of the Organisation of the Classroom

ORGANISING THE CLASSROOM SPACE	ORGANISING RESOURCES	CHILDREN'S NEEDS AND PREFERENCES
• Areas for teaching led activities through table layout, e.g. use of semi-circular table around whiteboard, rectangular table over non-carpeted areas. • The quiet room/space – used as a therapeutic space to take time out with soft toys and other activities Opportunities to utilise whole school resources, e.g. soft play, swimming, outdoors/trips, playground, gardening.	• Resources can be kept safely (locked in cupboards) Resources being clearly labelled for staff and child access: Use Alternative and Augmentative labelling, e.g. use of objects of reference, pictures and/or symbols on cupboards and drawers. Some resources will be accessed from outside the classroom: • Exchange resource list with other classes • Use knowledge of curriculum leads • Use equipment provided by the multi-disciplinary team (Speech and Language therapists, Occupational and Physiotherapists) Ensure resources, especially electronic ones, are not broken and are in working order	Children will see different staff members in different ways. There will be some that they feel more at ease with. This is particularly important for children with emotional difficulties. • Recognise that children may gravitate towards the adults they want to spend time with, e.g. play, engage with, etc. • Ask the child who they would like support from with the activities • Reduce child's anxiety by working with a preferred member of staff. Gradually increase child's resilience by working with a range of staff during structured and unstructured times

TABLE 2.3.2 Continued

THE CURRICULUM	ACTIVE AND INTERACTIVE TEACHING AND LEARNING	MULTI-SENSORY
The curriculum is based on the needs of the child and the skills and knowledge they have already learnt. All children should have a curriculum that ensures their Quality of Life as they move to adulthood. Important areas for their Quality of Life are these: • Communication • Mobility and accessing the environment • Empowerment through making choices • Building Relationships • Developing Independence Children (with a developmental age of under about 6 months) require a multisensory pre-symbolic curriculum that supports the quality of their life Children with a developmental age of under 24 months require a pre-academic play-based curriculum and the development of independence skills Children with a development age of over 24 months require an adapted Early Years Curriculum focussing on functional academic skills including reading, writing, mathematics and science and the development of independence skills. Children who become emotionally distressed may do so because the curriculum they are being asked to follow is too easy or too difficult. It is important to acknowledge the wide range of needs in the classroom. Consider this: • What are the right curriculum areas for this child? • Is there clarity about the outcomes in each curriculum area? • Are the lessons/activities in a group setting and 1:1 differentiated according to individual needs? • Does the child have difficulties that make engaging with this curriculum difficult/frustrating? • Does this child have strengths which make parts of the curriculum boring?	Traditionally, teaching involved teachers imparting knowledge through giving children' information either verbally or through directed reading. Our children are mostly taught skills through active learning where they must do something. This active learning should contain elements of play and fun. To do this, teaching is usually interactive in nature where the adult demonstrates or models an activity and then interacts with the child to support their involvement using physical and/or verbal guidance to support their engagement. For children with emotional difficulties both the active and the interactive aspects of this process may be difficult. **Consider how to engage children through the following:** • Activating children's interest, through developing initiative and choice making. • During Circle Time use visual aids, e.g. photographs of children and staff • Using children led activities for exploring the environment • Ensuring activities are fun – not threatening • Linking activities to music and singing • Linking activities to movement • Linking activities to role playing • Link activities to different media, e.g. cameras, tablets, PCs Learning is supported through interactive teaching. A range of strategies should be integrated into the day. **Consider how to do the following:** • Integrate interactive technology, e.g. whiteboards, computers, smart notebooks and the internet • Group teaching sessions based on interactive skills Recognise the constant evolution of individual needs and adapt strategies accordingly through discussion with the class team	Multi-sensory environments contain equipment that is designed to produce sensory stimulation. Sensory stimulation can be used for several purposes. Originally, they were designed to help children with leisure opportunities to relax. In that way they may be used to help children with emotional difficulties a space to calm down and relax. However, they are now often to promote sensory development through a sensory curriculum. Children's sensory development is tied to the idea of the development of communication and cognition. Personalised sensory soothing can be provided in many different areas and places, i.e. in and out of the classroom, on the bus and even on the child through a sensory belt. Sensory soothing needs to be child centred and tailored to the child's individual needs. However, it is important that children do not become fixated on one type of sensory soothing as a way of controlling their anxiety. **Consider why are you using sensory equipment?** • Are you using it for soothing or stimulation? • Does the multisensory environment/equipment fit with your use – soothing or stimulation? **Multisensory Environments:** **Dark room:** Light projectors, bubble tube, fibre optic strings **Sensory room:** tyres, large soft cushions, a stretch suit, Tacpac – multi-sensory set, access to substances (sand, fun soap, lentils, playdough, water etc.), activity arches **ICT: IWB** (sing along songs and Real books), stand-alone computers, switches and switch toys, software, tablets, iPad

TABLE 2.3.3 Sub-Categories of Teaching Strategies

DEMONSTRATING UNCONDITIONAL POSITIVE REGARD	USING INTENSIVE INTERACTION	AUGMENTATIVE AND ALTERNATIVE COMMUNICATION
The core of the relationship between the class team and the children is the concept of "unconditional positive regard". This is shown by two qualities: respect and empathy. **Respect** is about showing that the children matter. **Consider how the class team**<ul><li>Are appropriately affectionate to all children.</li><li>Use interactions as opportunities to develop affectionate relationships.</li><li>Model and practice appropriate ways to receive and show affection using touch, facial expressions (smiling) and tone of voice.</li><li>Show they are "for" the children</li><li>Assume the child's goodwill</li><li>Show they are competent</li><li>Remain calm and positive</li><li>Are positioned in the classroom to show availability to the children</li></ul>**Empathy** is the ability to see things from the child's point of view – to be able to walk in their shoes. **Consider how staff**<ul><li>Use Intensive Interaction to read and respond to any expressive signs the children give, no matter how small they are, for example sounds, facial expression or body language.</li><li>Use appropriate communication tools such as their PECS books, emotion symbols and Makaton.</li><li>Engage with children in their activities</li><li>Show interest in the children's lives – for example using visuals for what they did at the weekend.</li><li>Question children on how they are, how they have been and what they wish to do.</li><li>Engage in positive and trusting ways offering verbal reassurance and comfort.</li><li>Model how to express feeling.</li><li>Reassure when child is ill.</li><li>Develop and express emotions through creative arts, e.g. music, visual arts.</li></ul>	Intensive Interaction is an approach to teaching the fundamentals of interaction and communication. It has been successfully used with children with severe and complex learning difficulties who are still at an early stage of communication development. Intensive interaction is a fun process and helps the child and the staff team to relate better to each other and enjoy each other's company more. Intensive Interaction fosters children's emotional engagement with learning, and between the class team and the child. **Consider how the class team does the following:**<ul><li>Uses body language to signal their availability</li><li>Joins the child in their world and responds to them</li><li>Let's the child lead the interaction</li><li>Does not force or drive the interaction</li><li>Is playful – nothing specific must be achieved</li><li>Respects the child's rights – to stop or to go on</li><li>Is relaxed about repetition</li><li>Develops enjoyable and relaxed interaction sequences with the child.</li><li>Develops these interaction sequences in terms of duration, complexity and sophistication</li></ul>	Many children with learning difficulties use individual means of communication. "Augmentative and Alternative communication" is an umbrella term used to describe any system that aids the child to communicate. It can be divided into **unaided** such as using body language and signing and **aided** for example when the child uses PECS symbols or a computer to aid communication. Aided systems are often divided into high tech and low tech. High tech systems are based on electronic aids such as iPad. Low tech aids may simply rely on symbols or photos. **Consider how different systems are being used:** **Unaided:**<ul><li>Use of voice – tone, pitch, etc.</li><li>Drumming, call and response activities</li><li>Songs and music connected to daily routine</li><li>Pointing</li><li>Body language</li><li>Touch cues</li><li>Signing (e.g. Makaton)</li><li>Intensive interaction</li></ul>**Aided: Low Tech**<ul><li>Eye gaze board</li><li>"I want" chart</li><li>"Now/Next" board</li><li>Communication book</li><li>Objects of reference</li><li>Pictures/photos/symbols</li><li>PECS</li></ul>**Aided: High Tech**<ul><li>Use of technology, e.g. iPad</li><li>Use of specialised technology, e.g. Voice output communication aids</li><li>Switches</li><li>IWB</li></ul>Consider how children's responses/preferences are observed and responded to.

TABLE 2.3.4 Sub-Categories of Shared Communication Systems

BUILDING A WORKING ALLIANCE BETWEEN THE CHILDREN AND THE CLASS TEAM	BUILDING A RELATIONSHIP BETWEEN THE CHILDREN AND THE CLASS TEAM	BUILDING A RELATIONSHIP WITH PEERS
For children with emotional difficulties it is helpful to build a working alliance with them as the foundation for building a relationship. This alliance is based on your understanding of the child's emotional reactions to events in the classroom. Some children who are insecure will withdraw and not respond to adults' affection. Other insecure children can respond to affection by initially increasing their demands on adults and appearing hyperactive and out of control. Staff need to remain calm and consistently and repeatedly role model safe interactions. Children need to feel safe in order to build relationships. **Staff need to** • Respond at the moment the "child" arrives. • Greet the children happily at the start of each day. • Recognise and respond to how the child is feeling when they arrive at school. • Be approachable by all the children at all times and in all things. • Give children the opportunity to be with a one on one adult during activities, use personal prompts and intensive interaction. • Respond to attempts to initiate contact. • Use a range of structured communication systems to relate to the child. • Be good at "listening" to the children. • Repeat yourself time and time again. • Remain open minded to the children. • Show them that you have a sense of humour. • Start each day with a fresh start. Do not bear grudges. • Acknowledge and communicate with children that they do have "off days" and discuss how best to handle them.	The day needs to be organised so that there is a positive environment and that there are opportunities for the children to build a relationship with the class team. Children need to be encouraged to initiate interactions, communications and conversation. **Consider whether** • Adults work with all children to create opportunities for contact. • Adults promote/encourage children to initiate interactions during different activities throughout the day, e.g.: • During adult directed sessions • Free play/choosing time • Lunchtime/playtime • Specialist areas • Areas for directed learning • Adults acknowledge pointing or leading adults to an object they want or an activity they want to take part in. • Adults participate in activities that the child has chosen and finds interesting, e.g. chasing games. • During free play adults and children learn about each other, e.g. soft play. • Children are asked whom (from the class team) they would like to work with for morning work. • Adults dance with the children • Adults laugh with the children	Developing friendships with peers is an important aspect of developing relationships. Friendships developed in school may continue into adult life. Children need the opportunities in terms of time, space and skills to contact other children, in the classroom and around the school. It is important that children are given choice about who they are friends with. **Consider whether** • You know who children like in the class. • Children are asked to choose who they would like to sit, work and play with. • Children are encouraged to include others in their games / activities. • Friendships are built through shared interests and activities. • Friendships are built by putting children beside each other. • You use a buddy system in the class. • Children who play alongside their peers rather than interact, are encouraged to interact. • There is interaction during circle time and lessons. • During "hello", the children can respond when everyone sings "hello" to them. • During choosing time – there is not only the activity but a person to share it with. • Inclusion is planned – music and art with mainstream children. • When joint trips happen with other classes – children are asked to choose who they would like to walk and sit with. • Assemblies create opportunities. • Whole school activities; creative arts week, sports day. • Shared lunch and play time with other children in school. • Children get to choose what weekly jobs they want to do, and if they want to share that activity with someone else.

TABLE 2.3.5 Sub-Categories of Developing Relationships

COOPERATION AND COMMUNICATION	ORGANISATION OF ROLES	KNOWING THE CHILDREN
An effective team is more than a group of individual people. An effective team has synergy which gives it more strength and energy than everyone acting on their own. **Ensure the class team** - Respects, supports and are positive with each other throughout the school day. - Has daily discussion of issues and activities to increase levels of consistency and ensure clarity around all activities. - Holds weekly class meeting for feedback, reflection and discussion of the emotional needs of individual children and how to respond to them. - Uses staff experience to be able to support and respond to individual children's needs. - Holds weekly class meeting for planning the timetable for the next week. - Holds regular school staff meetings to ensure consistency and innovative practice across classrooms. - At meetings, values and listens to everyone's contribution and ensure fairness and openness to speak on issues of concern. - Continues to communicate formally/informally throughout the day. - Uses a variety of means of communication, e.g. whiteboard, post-its, emails. - Supports each other with regards to acquisition of new/different skills. - Celebrates success each day.	Each member of the class team will have different strengths and interests. In addition, they will relate differently to different children. It is important that these strengths are utilised not only because it will help the children's well-being but also the staffs' well-being. **Consider how** - The class team identifies which children they like to work with. - Key workers are assigned for each child. - Team members skills can be brought to particular activities and built into the timetable. - There is a clear organisation of roles, activities and responsibilities across class teams throughout the day, e.g. rotas for personal care, lunch support, taking children to buses. - Feedback is given to the next staff member who is working with a child. - Team members know it is OK to ask for help if they need support for a child.	In the same way that slight changes can affect a child's emotional well-being, small changes in behaviour can also indicate a child's emotional well-being. However, the classroom is a very busy place and even when the small change is noticed the pattern of engagement and relationship behind this change can go unnoticed. By close observation and good written records these changes can be more clearly identified. To understand the children's emotional well-being the class team should be producing a range of records. These records may be written, e.g. post-its, or visuals, e.g. photographs. Each member of the class team has a responsibility for observing the children, though actually it will be one person who records the progress. That person relies on the observations of all the other members of the team. **Consider how the class team** - Uses daily and weekly class team meetings to discuss the children's engagement in the curriculum, their relationships and their emotional well-being. - Plans for detailed observation of particular children. - Ensures special books, personal files, daily recording and monitoring forms are kept up to date. - Ensures individual profiles (behaviour, independence targets and communication) are updated and reflect the child's emotional well-being. - Displays the children's activities, achievements and reward charts. - Uses ABC charts to analyse and reflect on the child's behaviour and to plan strategies to help children feel safe and secure. - Shares observations including video clips with parents/carers.

TABLE 2.3.6 Sub-Categories of the Supportive Class Team

A SAFE CLASSROOM	A SAFE GROUP	TRANSITIONS IN SCHOOL

Children need to feel that the classroom is a safe space. This is maintained by setting clear expectations and boundaries for behaviour. Children need to know what these expectations are and to understand why they're in place. These can be set out as rules that are simple, clear and positive. They should serve as a reminder of what is expected rather than what is not accepted.
 	
Consider whether expectations for behaviour are
 	
- Discussed and agreed upon by the class team.
- Clear and in line with school policy and behaviour framework.
- Fairly and consistently applied (both over time and between staff).
- Communicated using clear and concise visual rules using words, symbols and pictures.
 	
Many behaviours can be simply managed using a graded and gradual response.
 	
Consider how you
 	
- Use positive praise to highlight strengths and to reinforce good behaviour.
- Use a variety of reinforcement strategies, e.g. reward charts and tokens.
- Plan to ignore certain behaviours.
- Say what you want, not what you don't want, e.g. use the expressions "be gentle" rather than "stop hitting/pinching".
- Are proactive and aware of where potential problems may arise, e.g. triggers, cues.
- Use verbal and physical strategies to prompt the child about appropriate behaviour.
	For many children, the most unpredictable part of the school day is the emotional reactions and behaviour of other children. Children with emotional difficulties often find it difficult being with children who are emotionally secure. They may take the feelings of hurt out on the secure child by biting, scratching or hitting them.
	
	Consider how you
	
	- Use Circle Time in the morning and afternoon to acknowledge how children are feeling in a safe and trusting space.
	- Encourage children to "speak" about feelings throughout the day using the "feeling boards".
	- Give children positive strategies to use instead of negative behaviours, e.g. instead of "Abi don't pull Helen, wait until she takes her coat off". Try "Abi help Helen take her coat off and then you can play together".
	- Use plenary and reflection time to celebrate participation and joint work.
	- Use class assemblies to strengthen the groups identity.
	- Use time outside class (swimming, class trips) to strengthen the groups identify.
	- Use whole school acknowledgement of achievements.
	
	If children do not feel safe (due, for example, to the unpredictability of other children in the class) this will make them anxious and/or aggressive. They may feel they cannot interact without fear of injury from the other children.
		Transition between settings or activities is problematic for many children with emotional difficulties. A transition means leaving something secure and manageable. To feel safe, the child needs to believe that the new setting or activity will not frighten and overwhelm them. Careful planning for key points of support during transition is essential.
		
		Consider how to
		
		- Ensure the transition into school each morning is regular and familiar.
		- Start each day with the same routine.
		- Ensure transitions during the school day are regular and familiar, e.g. from the classroom to the lunch hall.
		- Use communication throughout the day to prepare children for transition.
		- Use a range of activities throughout the day to support transitions including the following:
		  – "Now and Next" boards
		  – Music
		  – Countdowns
		  – Sand timers
		  – Favoured objects
		  – Transitional objects
		  – "Traffic Lights" system
		
		If children show anxiety during particular activities staff can offer reassurance, a short break then return to the activity or an opportunity to stop at or before the natural end of the activity. Less frequent transitions need even more careful planning to ensure children do not become anxious.

TABLE 2.3.7 Sub-Categories of Feeling Safe

A SAFE CLASSROOM	A SAFE GROUP	TRANSITIONS IN SCHOOL
When children become emotional upset, anxious or angry, the class team needs to apply consistent interventions depending on the individual needs of the child: • Use confident, calm and firm tone with children when applying strategic intervention. • Move the child away from a situation to support the child to calm down first and help them to feel safe. • Use positive physical intervention.	**Consider how** • Children are encouraged to move, change seats or to leave an activity or situation if they are feeling uncomfortable. • Children can indicate if they are distressed by the activity or another child, e.g. give a symbol to indicate their desire to move.	**Consider how you** • Use social stories to prepare children for new activities outside the classroom. • Inform children of timetable changes as soon as possible with corresponding changes to the class visual timetable. • Plan for transitions that include moving through areas of the school that may be anxiety provoking. • Recognise and plan for major points of transition with parents and other professionals, e.g. end of year, key stage, moving school. • Build relationships with other class teams for transitions at the end of the year.

TABLE 2.3.7 Continued

FEELING THE GOODWILL OF ADULTS	FEELING THE FRIENDSHIP OF PEERS	FEELING THE FAMILY LOVE
When secure children are distressed, they will usually turn to an adult as a safe haven to get emotional support and to help them regulate and contain their emotions. The staff team needs to offer comfort and support when children are emotionally upset. Adults need to listen to "children's voices" and become attuned to the daily changes of needs and emotional well-being. **Consider how you** • Welcome children as soon as they walk in the door. • Identify children's emotional state so that it can be responded to appropriately. • Show children they are being celebrated and kept in mind, i.e. photos, individual profiles, birthdays. • Use relaxing and comforting activities that will support children, e.g. relaxing music is played at start of each day. • Look for children's signs and triggers and try to understand and comprehend emotional distress before it happens. • Acknowledge that when children are distressed about something there is always a reason and it is important to be calm and responsive. • Help negotiate and resolve any immediate issues they may have.	For many children, especially teenagers, an emotional engagement with other children is often central to their own emotional well-being. If the child is secure in their relationships with their friends, they are likely to be more emotionally secure. It is important to build group cohesion through developing friendships and whole class identity. Understanding how to accept and show affection may initially need a great deal of modelling by staff with other staff. Not only do the children have communication difficulties, they also have cognitive difficulties which make it difficult for them to see the world from another person's point of view. The class team needs initially to draw attention to other children. **Consider how staff draw children's attention to each other:** • In the morning through greetings "Look James here's Gurpreet". • Comment positively on how children are dressed. • Comment on how they are looking – well, tired etc. • During register, comment on who is here and who is not. • Ask where children are. • Use emotion cards to ask how children are feeling. • Use emotion cards to ask children to think about how other children are feeling. Once this awareness is developed, attention can be turned to the interaction between children.	The home-school relationship is particularly important for children's emotional well-being. Children need to feel they are being emotionally held in both settings and between both settings. This requires a strong positive relationship between school staff and a child's family or primary carer. Parents need to know that the class team understand their child's needs and diagnosis. They also need to know that the class team understands and respects their culture and their roots. **Daily Communication** The key to developing a good relationship between school and home is daily communication. Daily communication ensures that parents/carers feel their needs and the needs of their child are known and responded to by staff. It also is how school staff show their care and support for the child. This communication can focus on the past, what they did, or on the future reminders of meetings or trips out. Communication can be done both face to face and indirectly. It can be done face to face through the following: • Direct contact at the beginning and end of the day for parents who bring their children to and from school • Class coffee mornings • Pastoral staff in school • Telephone calls It can be done indirectly through the following: • Communication book • Escorts • Emails and texts • Photos and drawings • Video links Communication helps parents to feel their child is safe and that the school cares about them. This daily communication may focus on a particular need of the child or on more general news. For example, if a child is finding the transition from home to school to be difficult, then this can be the focus of the communication. Parents can share why a pupil is having a difficult start to the day.

TABLE 2.3.8 Sub-Categories of Feeling Loved

FEELING THE GOODWILL OF ADULTS	FEELING THE FRIENDSHIP OF PEERS	FEELING THE FAMILY LOVE
• Offer comfort or support when children are distressed, e.g. hugs, massage and deep tissue pressure, reassuring words and gestures • Provide children with different choices if they are distressed, e.g. activities, places to be, adults to be with. • Offer time away from group when they are feeling distressed, e.g. in the "pod"/quiet room where they can go in on their own terms to get the sensory stimulation they need or to calm down. • Teach children how to self-regulate and relax.	**Consider how staff:** • Use a narrative dialogue across the day about who is doing what, who is playing with who, what peers are doing together. E.g. "Omar you are having a good time with your friend Oli". • Bring attention to the positive things' peers are doing together. • Give feedback which highlights how pupils are helping each other, e.g. "I saw James helping Helen with her numbers during maths, well done James". • When someone has returned from being away draw attention with a group greeting at the start of the session e.g. "Oh, I think Oli is finding this piece difficult, maybe Onur could help"	**Whole School Approaches** Schools should also have whole school approaches to building relationships with families. This is both an individual class team's responsibility as well as a whole school responsibility. Whole school approaches offer more opportunities for developing a supportive relationship between the school and families that secures engagement and builds understanding of the emotional needs of the child. **Consider how the following strategies are used:** • Whole school assemblies and events • Parents as volunteers in school • Coffee mornings for parents • Focussed workshops, e.g. communication, sleep, eating, behaviour • Problem-solving consultations with individual parents • Support for accessing services – filling in forms • Statutory meetings, e.g. annual reviews Sometimes it may be simply about parents having someone who will listen to them: i.e. knowing the school has an "open door policy" at the school management level, even if it is never used is the foundation of that trusting relationship.

TABLE 2.3.8 Continued

MAKING CHOICES	DEVELOPING INTERNAL MOTIVATION	BECOMING INDEPENDENT
Children feel confident and in control when they are given choices. Control is only meaningful when the choice made by the child is acted on. Only choices that are viable options should be offered so that adults can implement the child's choice. Child control is also a key to internal motivation and engagement. Lack of control can lead to anger and frustration by the child. Build the opportunities for giving control into the school day. Remember that if at any point in the day you must make a choice maybe that choice can be given to the child. **Consider how you** • Reduce the anxiety around making a choice, initially aim to offer a choice between two things. • Limit choice if child is emotionally overwhelmed. • Use the child's communication system (e.g. their PECS book) to choose an activity. • Give the child time to respond as making a choice can be emotionally difficult. • Ensure children are given the choice to continue with an activity, i.e. checking in with students "Finished or More?" using their communication system. Choices can be between objects (e.g. what to drink) or more often between activities. It can also be about the time spent on an activity or the sequence of doing activities (e.g. "Which do you want to do first?"). Choosing time around activities should be built into all children's daily timetable.	Internal and external motivation are best seen as on a continuum rather than as separate. Children's feelings of confidence can be supported by external motivation using rewards. Rewards are common in all schools and vary in their impact depending on what the child finds motivating. In an ideal world every child would be internally motivated and engaged. However, the reality is that once in school children have to do things that are socially required, are difficult, or take sustained effort. This is when external rewards are helpful to develop confidence. **Consider how you are using external rewards in class:** • Praising the child verbally, singing "bravo", clapping. • Praising the child using symbols or tokens (e.g. a happy face, a star). • Praise the child using role models of people they admire, or from familiar TV programmes (e.g. Mr Tumble, Spartacus). • Show work and congratulate each other at the end of sessions or the day. • Award "star of the week" in class. • Give the child of the week acknowledgement, e.g. leads circle time, snack time or a visit to the headteacher. • Present the certificate in Assembly. • Write positive messages (and/or stickers) in home/school book. • Put their work on display. • Present a video of themselves. It is important to develop the child's internal motivation. Internal motivation is a critical component of the quality of a child's life and is tied to becoming confident and independent and being able to make choices. Developing internal motivation is based on three factors; autonomy, competence and relatedness.	As children become more independent, they develop their feelings of confidence. This is particularly true for children with learning difficulties who are more likely to be dependent on others throughout their lives. Being able to look after yourself is central to feeling confident. The class team should get to know the "mantra" of each child and use it in the classroom. Don't block the natural rhythm a child has. Let the child show their confidence and lead into what they want. Work with the parents to encourage independence at home. **Consider how to develop their skills for independent living:** • Children are given opportunities to make choices throughout the day to develop independence skills both in and out of the classroom. • Children are involved in setting their own individual targets for developing their independence skills. • Children are given choice about where they want to sit at snack time and lunchtime and what they want to eat. • At playtime, swimming and P.E. they get dressed/undressed and decide on appropriate clothing. • During personal care time children decide when to go to the toilet and take care of their needs independently.

TABLE 2.3.9 Sub-Categories of Feeling Confident

MAKING CHOICES	DEVELOPING INTERNAL MOTIVATION	BECOMING INDEPENDENT
Consider if • On completion of a set activity children can choose from a range of activities for a brief period as a motivator. • In choosing time a child can choose to end or change an activity when they wish. • Children can continue with activities if they have shown a desire to do a part of the activity for longer than was initially planned. • Some sessions are organised into short activities where the children can participate, allowing for a choice of movement breaks. Group: • Children can choose who to work with • Children can choose who would like to start if sharing ideas in the group Whole class: • Timetable opportunities outdoors or indoors for choosing activities • Allow opportunities to choose what activity the whole class may do together that day Choice is crucial to developing Internal Motivation	**Consider how to ensure the following:** 1. **Autonomy** – what choice and control do children have over their activities? E.g. • Giving them a choice after completing an activity • Gearing the curriculum to the child's interests 2. **Competence** – does the classroom make the child feel competent? • Is the task set at a level where they can finish the task? • Can they complete an additional extension activity? • Could they show their completed activity to their peers or staff? 3. **Relatedness** – do the children feel that the staff care about their activities and progress? e.g. • Show an interest in the child when they are involved in free play. • Comment on their play. • Praise the children for their effort during their activity. • Spontaneously acknowledge children for their positive interaction with you.	**Consider how you give more responsibility to the children:** • Children decide whether outdoor or indoor play is more appropriate depending on the timetable or weather. • Set out snacks. • Wash and clear up. • Through modelling and role play children can get the resources they need for a learning session, on their own. • Use drama, role play and dressing up to try out different roles. • Give each child a turn to be "teacher". • Use self-evaluation – using symbols for evaluating whether something was good/bad, easy/hard, happy/sad.

TABLE 2.3.9 Continued

Section 3
Supporting an individual child

Understanding an individual child

Introduction

Developing the Emotionally Supportive Classroom, as described in Section 2, is designed to nurture the emotional well-being of all the children in the classroom and across the school. It is important that this is firmly embedded before moving on to providing targeted support for individual children. However, no matter how effective these classroom strategies are there will still be children and young people whose emotional well-being you remain concerned about. This section provides a means for class teams and the whole school to understand, identify and support individual children with emotional difficulties.

The whole school and class teams can support the individual child through the four phases described in this section. These phases should be tackled sequentially. However, often it will not be necessary to go through all four phases for an individual child. Sometimes simply completing Phase 1 will provide class teams with enough understanding of how to support the child.

The four phases are these:

Phase 1: Understanding the reasons for the emotional difficulties of an individual child

Phase 2: Understanding the extent of the emotional difficulties of an individual child

Phase 3: Developing class-based solutions using Solution Circles

Phase 4: Developing community-based solutions using the multi-agency team and Quality Circles

Each of these phases is dealt with by a separate chapter in this section of the book.

Musa

Musa, a ten-year-old little boy will be used as an example throughout this section to illustrate the process. The child you are concerned about may have very different difficulties. So, the examples with Musa simply illustrate the process – they do not provide solutions to your concerns.

Supporting an individual child

> In your classroom there is a 10-year-old boy, Musa. Musa becomes distressed very easily – numerous times throughout the day. When he is distressed he will try to hit, scratch and/or kick adults and other children who are near him. When he is physically restrained he becomes very angry and will try to bite himself and others whilst resisting any form of restraint. It takes him a long time to settle down once he becomes upset. What can you do?

EXAMPLE 3.1.1 Musa

There are no simple solutions for children like Musa. However, the first step is to try to understand why he is emotionally so fragile and is so prone to these outbursts. It may be possible to identify some triggers for these outbursts and addressing these may initially reduce the frequency of his outbursts. However, over time what is most likely to happen is that you simply change the trigger to something else. To understand why Musa is becoming so distressed you need to address the causes, not just the symptoms, and take a long-term approach. His distress and emotional difficulties are not going to change overnight. His understanding of the world and emotional responses have developed over the first 10 years of his life and it is reasonable to expect that it will take him several years to learn how to manage his emotions and not to become so emotionally distressed. This does not mean that you can't help him in the short term – you can.

It is helpful to start by thinking about this emotional distress from his point of view. If Musa can talk you can ask him – however as he has severe learning difficulties this may be very difficult. So instead you have to imagine what he might say.

> What would Musa say if you asked him why he became so distressed and hits and bites others?
> He would say:
> - I don't understand what you want me to do
> - I don't want to do what you want me to do
> - I feel trapped and frightened
> - I can't make you understand how I feel

EXAMPLE 3.1.2 Musa's Perspective

Musa probably would not know what made him distressed and would certainly not be able to articulate his feelings. You must try and imagine yourself in his shoes.

> Think of a child whose emotional well-being is causing you concern. If they could say why they became so upset and distressed what would they say?
> They would say:

ACTIVITY 3.1.1 What Would the Child Say?

So why do children with severe and complex learning difficulties become so emotionally distraught? The most important theory in helping to understand the emotional well-being of all children – including those like Musa – is Attachment theory. Attachment theory was developed over 50 years ago by the British psychologist John Bowlby (Bowlby, 1969, 1988). Though sometimes criticised, the theory has evolved over time and is now seen as a powerful way of understanding, and helping, children with emotional difficulties and mental health problems. Attachment is conceptualised as a primary evolutionary-based instinct that is in place to protect a child from harm. Essentially it is the feelings and behaviours that are activated when a child feels unsafe or threatened. When a young child feels unsafe, they become anxious and distressed – and depending on their previous experiences may have difficulty soothing and calming themselves. Attachment theory predicts that, when a child feels anxious and distressed, they will turn to an adult to make them feel safe.

The original focus of Attachment theory was on the relationship children have with their mothers as their main carers. It is now recognised that there are other relationships which also affect the development of attachment. These bonds are with other members of the family, including the child's father and grandparents, and also relationships with other significant adults – including staff in playgroups, nurseries and schools. Because of the importance of secure attachment in terms of emotional well-being, school staff are significant in supporting children's mental health. At the most basic level school staff can provide security in terms of predictability and calmness – especially in what can otherwise be a confusing and threatening world for the child with severe and complex learning difficulties.

There are several reasons that could make children with severe and complex learning difficulties feel particularly vulnerable and insecure. By understanding these reasons, you are in a better position to develop a strategy to help support children like Musa. The Fishbone diagram (Diagram 3.1.1) highlights four key factors that affect children with severe learning difficulties. This helps us to recognise the difficulties an individual child may face. There may be other factors or reasons that an individual child feels vulnerable or insecure. These can be shown in the diagram as additional spines on the Fishbone. The diagram is a powerful tool in exploring all the known factors that are impacting on a child's emotional well-being.

Factor 1: separation from caregivers

One of the primary causes of attachment difficulties for any child is when they are separated from their mother, or main caregivers, in the first few years of their life. Unfortunately, this is what happens to many children with severe and complex learning difficulties. This may happen if they spend time in hospital as a small baby

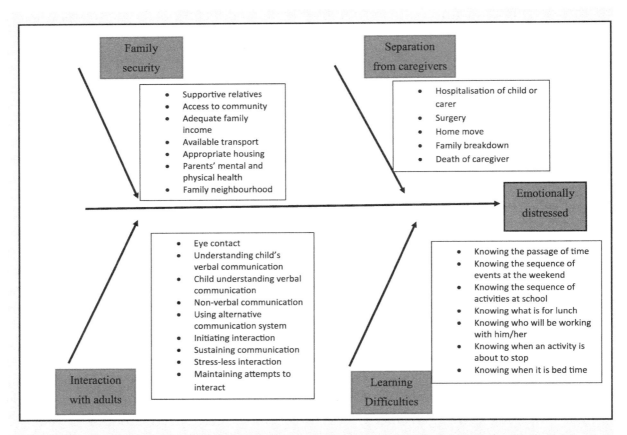

Diagram 3.1.1 The Fishbone of Factors that Affect the Development of Emotional Well-Being

and toddler. Sometimes this is due to a premature birth, or it may be due to illness or medical complications in their early life. This often results in the baby being separated from their mother or main carer at this very vulnerable stage of their early emotional development.

There are other reasons apart from medical why early separation may happen. There may be geo-political reasons, for example, when a family moves to the UK or relocates from one part of the UK to another. This may mean the child is separated from one, or both, of their parents for a few months or for a longer period. These periods of separation may, though not inevitably, cause feelings of insecurity. It is important that no blame is ascribed to the parents in these scenarios – as indeed no blame is attached to the doctors for their medical interventions. Unfortunately, these early separations from parents and other caregivers can have a significant impact on the child's emotional well-being. However, as will be discussed in the next section, the birth of a child with severe and complex learning difficulties is an unexpected and life-changing event which has an immediate impact on the security of the whole family.

Understanding an individual child

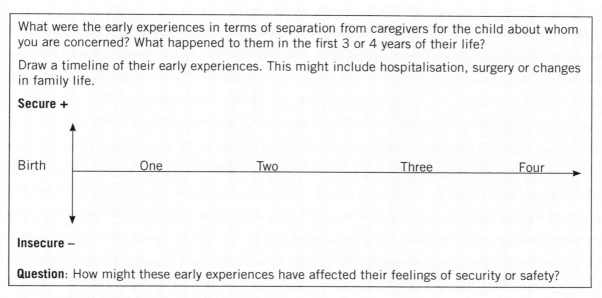

Activity 3.1.2 Separation from Caregivers

Factor 2: family security/relationships

The second key factor also helps explain why the child may have difficulties building a secure view of the world. This factor captures how the whole family's security and relationships are affected by the unexpected event of having a child born with a severe or complex need. Research shows how the family of a child with severe or complex needs finds that their time, energy and finances are significantly affected (Whiting, 2014). Some of the critical things that are affected are these:

- Relationships in the family
- The families' income
- Income and expenditure

Having a child with a disability is usually an unexpected event for the parents and many find it difficult to readjust their lives. The incidence of relationship breakdown for these families is higher than the national average. Parents of children with severe and complex needs are also known to be at higher risk of developing mental health issues themselves – often in the form of depression.

The ongoing and additional needs of the child with severe or complex needs often means that there is a drop in the family income. This may be because there is now only one income coming in as one parent must use all their time looking after the child. For example, poor sleep patterns are very common, requiring a parent to be awake frequently and/or for long periods during the night. Parents often comment how they take the opportunity to rest or catch up on sleep when their child is at school.

Having a child with severe learning difficulties also means an increase in expenditure. This include increased costs for example in terms of laundry, clothes, transport, heating, additional child care and other bills. It can cost three times as much to bring up a disabled child as it does a non-disabled child. Families of children with severe and complex learning disabilities often slide into poverty as a result of the lack of income and increased expenditure (Every Disabled Child Matters, 2007).

Obviously, these issues do affect other families, but they are more likely to happen to the families of children who have severe and complex needs. One way these difficulties can be minimised is through community resources in terms of the opportunity structures that support the whole security of the family. Recognising and promoting these resources also helps the emotional well-being of the children (Seligman & Darling, 2009).

Find out a little more about the family life of the child whose emotional well-being is causing you concern.
Common factors that reduce stress and give security are listed here.
Rate each of these factors for the family.

	VERY GOOD	QUITE GOOD	QUITE POOR	VERY POOR
Supportive Relatives and Community				
Access to Facilities, e.g. Playground, Shops				
Adequate Family Income				
Available Transport				
Appropriate Housing				
Parents' Mental and Physical Health				
Family Neighbourhood				

Comments:

Activity 3.1.3 Family Security/Relationships

Factor 3: Interaction with adults

How adults respond to a young child's attempts for reassurance when they feel unsafe (anxious) shapes the development of the child's attachment system – their emotional well-being. Two fundamental types of attachment can develop: secure and insecure.

- The child feels secure when they know an adult is available who will reduce their anxiety

- The child feels insecure when they are not certain that an adult is available to reduce their anxiety

All parents wish to develop a good relationship with their children and make them feel emotionally safe. However, the first two factors, already outlined, highlight largely environmental issues that may get in the way of this process. This next factor highlight's one of the difficulties in building relationships, which is directly affected by the child's severe and complex learning difficulties.

Research has identified the interactional difficulties there are when building a relationship with a child with a disability (Howe, 2006). These fundamentally stem from their learning difficulties but may also include physical and sensory issues. The difficulties in the child's ability to express emotion like other children can also have an impact on the parent-child relationship. A parent may long for a hug or an expression of love towards them which is not always possible. The child's difficulties with interaction may include the child having limited, or no, speech, difficulties with physical movement such as turning to an adult and difficulties reaching and touching making their interaction with caregivers and peers challenging. They may also have difficulties making and retaining eye contact or seeing what an adult is presenting to them. It may be particularly problematic for the child to initiate and get the adults' attention, and to sustain interactions with adults in order to play games. These interactions are the usual ways that the relationship develops between the parents and child – and for the child with severe and complex learning difficulties this becomes problematic.

Think of a child whose emotional well-being is causing you concern.
What difficulties do they have in sustaining interactions with you?
Rate the following factors

FACTOR	NO DIFFICULTIES	SOME DIFFICULTIES	GREAT DIFFICULTIES
Turning towards you			
Moving to be with you			
Making and retaining eye contact			
Seeing what you are showing them			
Getting your attention through initiating interaction			
Understanding your communication – verbal and non-verbal			
Using an alternative communication system			
Maintaining your interest and sustaining communication			

Question: What other interactional difficulties affect this child's ability to make relationships?

Activity 3.1.4 Interactions

Factor 4: learning difficulties

Through early experiences all children develop, inside their head, a dynamic and active understanding of themselves. John Bowlby (1988) called this the internal working model (IWM). The IWM contains the child's beliefs and expectations about the following:

- My value – am I lovable?
- My independence – am I capable and not dependent on adults?
- Your trustworthiness – will you ensure I am safe and secure?
- Your responsiveness – will you be responsive and help me to calm (regulate) my emotions if I become distressed?

The IWM is not fixed at birth for a child but develops through their interactions with caregivers – and particularly through their experiences when they are anxious and distressed. So, it may be that for 95% of the time the child is not separated from their caregivers, that the family is secure, and interactions are sustained and positive. However, it will be the adults' ability to calm the child when they are particularly anxious or distressed for that other 5% of the time that will become central to their internal working model.

A child uses this internal working model when they are anxious, distressed or during other emotionally charged situations. In these situations, a child must process two types of information:

- **Cognitive information**: to feel safe and secure a child must feel the world is predictable. For example, that certain events follow known previous events. A child needs to think that if they do X then Y will follow. However, for a child with severe or complex learning difficulties the world can appear very unpredictable. For example, they may not know when they leave the classroom whether they are going to lunch, or going swimming or going home? This uncertainty at a moment of transition can cause a child to feel unsafe and lead to a strong emotional reaction.
- **Emotional information**: to feel safe and secure, children, when they feel anxious or distressed, need to feel that their anxiety can be contained by the adults around them. Their internal working model should reassure them that, if they become upset, there are adults who will keep in check their feelings of anxiety or distress. Adults can do this by showing the children that no matter how distressed they are that they, the adult will remain calm and in control. However, as illustrated by the Fishbone, for a child with severe or complex learning difficulties there can be significant difficulties forming strong relationships with adults.

> Think of a child whose emotional well-being is causing you concern. What difficulties do they have knowing the world is predictable? Consider the following:
>
> - Knowing the passage of time
> - Knowing the sequence of events at the weekend
> - Knowing the sequence of activities at school
> - Knowing what they are going to have for lunch
> - Knowing which members of the class team will be working with them
> - Knowing when an activity is about to stop
> - Knowing when it is bedtime
>
> Question: What can they predict with certainty?

Activity 3.1.5 Cognitive Information

If a child feels that the world is predictable and that adults are willing and able to help reduce their levels of distress and anxiety then, over time, the child will internalise those experiences to form their own secure internal working model. This secure IWM enables the children to self-soothe and to develop the skills to be able to reduce their own levels of anxiety and distress. Over time this becomes an important condition in maintaining self-control. The IWM implies a dynamic process that helps a child make predictions about an adult's behaviour and the "dangers" within the environment. It operates outside conscious awareness and is revised with repeated and new experiences. All children are involved in a constructive process, actively trying to make sense of the situations they are in and over time building successful ways of emotionally responding to events as they occur.

Most children gradually learn that they can regulate their own emotions and can soothe and calm themselves. These children have developed secure attachments. For children with severe and complex learning difficulties, their early experiences, such as separation from carers, insecurity in the family, interactional difficulties and their cognitive limitations means the world is more likely to continue to be unpredictable. All these factors affect a child's ability to feel secure and they may develop an IWM which maintains feelings of insecurity and the inability to self- regulate their emotions. The child's IWM may then generate ways of emotionally responding which do not produce positive interactions with adults, thus perpetuating a negative and unsafe emotional cycle.

Complete Activity 3.1.6 on a child whose emotional well-being is causing you concern. Identify the factors which shape their IWM and makes them feel insecure and vulnerable? Identifying these factors may help you to understand why the child becomes so emotionally unstable and distressed. You may feel that you have little control over these factors – and some of them may have happened a long time ago. However, the IWM is dynamic and can be changed by what is happening in the here and now – that is, what you and the class team do daily.

Supporting an individual child

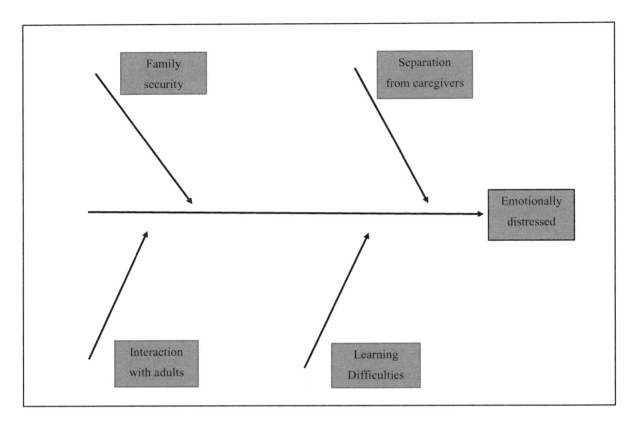

ACTIVITY 3.1.6 The Fishbone of Factors that Affect the Development of Emotional Well-Being

How insecure children react to their anxiety

Attachment theory distinguishes between two common strategies that the insecure child has to reduce anxiety – to withdraw or to intensify their distress.

Withdraw: some children learn that the best thing to do when feeling unsafe or insecure is to shut-down or withdraw emotionally. This may happen if a child has learnt that they are "on their own" when they are emotionally upset. It is as if they have learnt that "the only one who is going to keep me safe is me". A child may become emotionally closed and hide their emotion from others (and from themselves). This will occur when they believe that seeking support from adults is not possible and the best way to reduce stress is to become emotionally detached.

Intensify: some children learn that the safest thing to do is to intensify their emotional reactions. A child may maintain a state of constant emotional hyper-arousal and shows perpetual signs of distress, irritability and anger. This may occur when a child has learnt that seeking emotional support may lead to reassurance but may also lead to an emotional rejection or rebuffal. The child's IWM tells them that they should magnify or intensify their emotional demands in order to receive emotional support.

These two strategies also appear to be linked to gender, girls are more likely to withdraw, and boys are more likely to intensify their demands (Hamblin, 2016). Class teams are, understandably, more concerned about children – usually the boys – who intensify their demands. These are the children who appear emotionally and behaviourally out of control and potentially pose a physical threat not only to those around them but also to themselves. But it is important to also recognise how the children who are very quiet and withdrawn also have emotional problems and may be the ones who develop into depressed adults, with the additional risks of addiction and other self-destructive behaviours.

Common strategies to reduce anxiety

Common and appropriate strategies to develop a more secure IWM are based on three psychological processes:

- Boundaries – providing predictable and stable structures
- Holding – being available and responsive to the child
- Containing – the child's and your own emotions

School staff use these three strategies automatically – even if they do not describe them in these words. All these three processes involve the school staff in providing an emotionally caring and protective space which allows the child to learn how to feel safe and secure by themselves.

Think of a time when you were feeling insecure. This is likely to have been in a new situation. For example, being in a new job or being in a strange place (on holiday) or trying to learn to do something new (how to swim), or in a new relationship.
Questions: How did you feel: e.g. distressed, anxious, angry, numb?
How would the following have helped?

- Boundaries – Having clearer boundaries about what was expected, what you should do, where you could go?
- Holding – Having someone there who could answer your questions and address your worries?
- Containing – Having someone there who was calm and appeared to be in control and to know what they were doing?

ACTIVITY 3.1.7 Feeling Insecure

Boundaries

Boundaries are reliable and predictable structures. They set limits or "lines" that are not to be crossed and keep children feeling safe.

Boundaries include time frames that set out the structure of the day, the timing of activities and when they are going to start and end.

Boundaries also include the activities that the child can, and cannot, do. Access to activities may also be connected to time frames. A child may be allowed to kick a ball at playtime but not when they arrive at the beginning of the school day. Boundaries incorporate conventions, such as rules about the interaction with others, including other children and staff. Once again, these conventions may include time frames, e.g. it is OK to hold hands going into the hall but not at other times of the day.

Boundaries are largely developed and maintained through verbal instructions about what the children can and cannot do. These may be supported by physical prompts in terms of taking children's hands and guiding them to particular places or activities. They can be further supported using signs, symbols, gestures, objects of reference and/or transitional objects.

All boundaries require predictable consequences. The gambler will place a bet even if they are unsuccessful 19 times out of 20. Some children are gamblers – they will try to kick the football inside the classroom – even if 19 times out of 20 they are stopped. They only remember the 20th time. For some children every change is a new and challenging experience, even when it is a regular and routine activity that they may have done many times before.

> So, what for Musa are the boundaries that he needs to feel secure and safe? To begin with he needs to know:
>
> What will happen when he gets off the bus?
> Who will meet him and take him into school?
> Where will he go in the school?
> When will he get there?
> What will happen next?
> ...and so on for every change throughout the day

EXAMPLE 3.1.3 Boundaries for Musa in the Classroom

Holding

The best depiction of holding comes from the image of a mother holding her sobbing child in her arms and allowing them to express their emotions while making them feel safe. Gradually the child's sobbing subsides, and they realise that they have been able to calm themselves down. Initially the mother "holds" and helps to make sense of all the child's emotions. The child feels part of their mother, who processes the child's emotions and "returns" them in a modified and manageable way. The mother gradually allows the child to feel they can manage their emotions. Over time, the child learns that they can be upset and anxious by themselves – and still be safe. In this way the child gradually learns to manage and contain their own emotions. This holding environment facilitates the child's transition to emotional autonomy.

Some children with severe and complex learning difficulties may not have gone through this experience of having a consistent holding process with their mothers or other main caregivers. This may be for many of the reasons related to the four key factors on the fishbone (see Diagram 3.1.1). This means that when they become distressed, they do not feel that there is anyone who can comfort, reassure or make them feel safe. Once they become upset or angry it is very difficult to soothe them and to help them to calm down emotionally.

For these children, the class team needs to recreate a holding environment. This may not involve the actual physical holding of a child, but it will certainly mean an adult being physically close to the child. It will also mean being with the child when they are distressed – talking to them, reassuring them and showing them that you are empathetic and attuned to their emotional needs. For the distressed child, school staff need to be robust, reliable and trustworthy. By doing this you actually hold the child's anxiety and anger until they learn that they can emotionally survive without the immediate reassurance of adults.

However, the child is also likely to test out your holding capacity. They will instinctively challenge you to see how you react – whether you remain empathetic or whether you become angry and upset yourself. The more insecure the child feels the more they will challenge your holding capacity in order to try to feel safe.

> How would you "hold" Musa when he is anxious and distressed? Would you
>
> - Stand beside him – give him physical reassurance?
> - Soothe him by talking?
> - Find out what distressed him?
> - Make appropriate responses?
> - Understand what he is feeling?
>
> What else could you do to "hold" his distress?

EXAMPLE 3.1.4 "Holding" Musa in the Classroom

Containing

All children start off without boundaries or the experience of a holding environment. Most experience these in the first few years of their lives and begin to learn how to contain and control their emotions. We can see the development of this control in toddlers as they move from their "terrible two's" to becoming positive and engaged pre-schoolers at nurseries. However, some children miss these experiences and remain stuck as "terrible two's", overwhelmed by their own emotions. They have not developed sufficient internal control not to feel anxious and distressed. An adult's containing function involves helping the child develop a capacity for self-regulation. You need to be able to contain the child's emotional distress and return these emotions to the child in a modified, palatable form. The child needs to sense your emotional availability and your capacity to deal with their emotions in order to feel safe and contained. They will then eventually develop their own capacity to do the same.

So, school staff need to be able to contain their own emotions as well as those of the children. You may feel an overwhelming emotional reaction to a child's distress. This reaction may be feelings of anger, or helplessness, of anxiety or powerlessness and depression that you don't feel able to help. School staff are in a really difficult position. You need to be able to empathise with the child and to be attuned with their feelings while at the same time remaining calm and collected as an adult. The child's emotional distress can be transferred to the adult so that in the end you end up as distressed if not more distressed than they are.

How do you feel when Musa hits, bites or hurts another child or team member? Do you feel:
- Nothing
- Angry
- Worried
- Confused
- Anxious
- Helpless
- Frustrated

How do you contain your emotions?

Example 3.1.5 Containment for the Class Team

In order to support and address the emotional well-being of children with severe or complex learning difficulties, the emotional needs of the school staff and class teams must also be supported. School staff need to be engaged, have supportive relationships and to feel positive if they are going to be able to contain the emotional distress of the children. One of the key functions of the EWB coordinator is to ensure that the emotional well-being of the school staff is looked after – as well as the children.

Attachment theory and the difficulties of developing a secure internal working model provide ways of understanding why many children with severe and complex learning difficulties become so emotionally over-reactive and distressed. The next chapter describes how this directly affects Engagement, Relationships and Feeling Positive.

Understanding the extent of the emotional difficulties of an individual child

The Individual Profile of Emotional Well-Being

The Individual Profile of Emotional Well-Being provides a way refining your understanding of the emotional difficulties of an individual child. The Profile provides you with a means to assess the extent of the emotional difficulties. It identifies which, if any, of the three key areas of Engagement, Relationships and Feeling Positive are of particular concern, and what are the issues within these areas. The Individual Profile does not use medical or psychiatric terms to describe any mental health difficulties, such as the child being anxious, depressed, angry or psychotic. Instead the child's emotional well-being and mental health problems are grouped under the three areas where these problems can have an impact – Engagement, Relationships and Feeling Positive

The Individual Profile provides a list of constructs under each of these headings. The statements on the left of the profile all indicate positive emotional well-being (good mental health) while those on the right of the rating scale indicate areas for concern. The scaling means that each construct is seen as a continuum where it is possible to move, over time, from the higher scores on the right to the lower scores on the left. Using the profile in this way allows class teams to identify and agree on a focus for what can be done to address a child's emotional difficulties. A score can be assigned to each of the key areas – Engagement, Relationships and Feeling Positive by adding the rating of each construct within the key area. By adding the scores for all three areas together you have an overall indication of the severity of a child's emotional difficulties.

The Individual Profile was developed through feedback from staff in schools for children with severe and complex needs about the emotional well-being of individual children. The staff were asked to rate children on a series of constructs – with one end indicating the staff had no concerns about the child's emotional difficulties and the other end indicating that they had significant concerns. During this process, some constructs were omitted as they did not clearly discriminate between those children with, or without, emotional difficulties. New constructs were added, based on the experiences of school staff which were not being reflected in the original constructs. In addition, for some constructs the approach of the Coventry Grid (Moran, 2010) was used to distinguish between the emotional reactions of children with ASD and those with attachment difficulties.

Supporting an individual child

When to complete the Individual Profile

The most useful time to complete the Individual Profile is when you want to plan a support strategy for a child. You will already have identified your concerns about the child's emotional well-being and completing the profile will provide help in deciding on which of the three areas you focus your support.

There are several indicators that may also lead you to complete the Individual Profile.

1. Emotional responses are intense and persistent:

   The child's emotions are at the extremes, i.e. they are very emotionally withdrawn or over reactive.

   Questions to answer:

   - Is the child displaying emotional reactions such as crying or anger that are out of keeping with the situation?
   - Is the child very withdrawn and not communicating or interacting with their peers or staff?
   - Does the child find it very difficult to focus or attend to any activity even when they have a choice of activities?
   - How stable are these reactions over time?

2. Emotional responses have changed:

   This signals that something may have happened that has upset or scared the child emotionally.

   Questions to answer:

   - Are there changes to their sleeping or eating patterns?
   - Are there changes to their health, their posture or mobility?
   - What has happened at school that preceded or followed this change, e.g. new TA (Teaching Assistant), change of peer group?
   - What has happened at home that preceded or followed this change, e.g. hospitalisation, new baby, redundancy, ill health at home?

3. Emotional responses are consistent across situations:

   This signals that the child's emotional difficulties are not linked to one situation, but rather they have an internal difficulty with their emotions.

Questions to answer:

- Are these emotional responses occurring across most settings – home and school?
- Are these changes in emotional well-being occurring in different settings in school, e.g. the classroom, the playground?
- Are there any situations or places where these emotional reactions do not occur?

4   Parents or carers are very concerned:

Parents know their child best. If parents come with any of the aforementioned concerns, completing the Individual Profile will help identify what are the particular issues.

Questions to answer:

- Are parents very stressed?
- Do parents feel they are powerless to help their child emotionally?
- Are parents frustrated by their inability to successfully communicate with their child?
- Are parents worried that they cannot soothe their child?

(Adapted from Pappas & Frize, 2010. The Intellectual Disability Mental Health First Aid Manual. The National Association for Special Schools, 2007)

How to complete the Individual Profile

The Individual Profile can simply be completed by the class teacher. However, by following the process outlined here, you can obtain more useful information which will help when developing a strategy of support.

1   The Individual Profile should be completed on an individual child by the class teacher (or another team member) based on their own observations and experiences.

2   Once it has been completed, a second member of the staff team should also complete it – without seeing the first staff member's ratings – i.e. blind.

3   If this is not possible, then it can be completed by the same member of staff after a month.

4   Both sets of ratings are valid – there are no right or wrong answers.

Supporting an individual child

5   Staff should then examine the profile for the similarities and differences between the ratings.

6   Any variability either over time, or between different members of staff can be identified.

7   Differences in scoring at this stage are not unexpected and can become the basis for understanding how different adult interactions can affect a child's emotional well-being.

THE INDIVIDUAL PROFILE OF EMOTIONAL WELL-BEING

Name _____ Class _____ Date completed _____

ENENGAGEMENT	1	2	3	4	5	
Adapts and extends activities						Unable to adapt and extend activities
Continues to maintain interest over time						Loses interest quickly
Focuses on activity						Not motivated/aimless actions
Shows eager anticipation of an activity they have enjoyed before						No evident anticipation of a previously enjoyed activity
Aware they can impact on what happens next						Show no awareness of what happens next
Plays spontaneously						Requires cueing and prompting to engage
Engages in imaginative and symbolic play						Only engages in concrete play
Enjoys challenging activity						Disengages from challenging activity
New and different toys appreciated						Preference for old familiar toys **or** May destroy emotionally significant toys
Total Score:						

RELATIONSHIPS	1	2	3	4	5	
Seeks out adults for positive interaction						Does not seek out positive interaction
Emotional distress is soothed by adults						Adults unable to soothe distress

Understanding emotional difficulties

RELATIONSHIPS	1	2	3	4	5	
Can calm own emotions						Not able to calm own emotions
Shows sympathetic responses to others						Does not show sympathetic response to others
Develops new ways of interacting by observing others						Ways of interacting remains unchanged
Enjoys physical proximity						Dislikes physical proximity **or** Seeks excessive closeness when anxious
Interacts positively with adults						Avoids interactions with adults **or** Seeks to 'wind up' adults
Responds positively to adult attention						Does not respond positively to adult attention
Enjoys playing with other children						Prefers playing alone **or** Tries to impose on others when playing
Total Score:						

FEELING POSITIVE	1	2	3	44	45	
Has fun smiles and laughs						Is unhappy, dejected, withdrawn
Uses sound positively						Uses sound negatively (screams/screeches)
Makes good eye contact						Avoids eye contact
Responds positively to others						Responds negatively to others
Happy to attempt new activities						Reluctant to attempt new activities
Expresses wide range of emotions						Shows little or no emotion
Copes well with change						Becomes distressed/withdrawn by change
Interested in what is going on around them						Disinterested in what is going on around them
Settled positive mood						Sudden mood changes in respect to perceived injustices **or** Sudden mood changes related to internal state and perceived demands
Total Score:						
Total Score for all three areas:						

ACTIVITY 3.2.1 The Individual Profile of Emotional Well-Being

Interpretation of the individual child profile of emotional well-being

The Individual Profile does not have a cut off score between children who have emotional or mental health difficulties and those who have none. Instead emotional difficulties are seen on a continuum. The profile serves as a way of understanding the severity of a child's emotional needs compared with other children with severe and complex learning difficulties.

Children identified by their class teachers as having emotional difficulties usually have a total score of between 75–105 (average 90). As scores rise above 90 the class team should recognise the increasing severity of the child's difficulties.

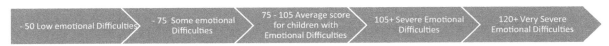

Figure 3.2.1 Rating Scale for Individual Child Profile

There are usually clear similarities between the total score in each of the three areas (within four points of each other). In other words, there is a link between all three areas when it comes to emotional difficulties. The average score for children whose teachers have identified as having emotional difficulties is therefore 30 or over in each of the three areas. These children have **general** emotional difficulties – therefore support in any of the three areas will affect the other two.

However, there are a small number of children identified with severe emotional difficulties who have considerable differences between their scores in the three areas (over 12 points difference between one or more of the areas). These children can be considered to have **specific** emotional difficulties. Support should focus on the area where the child is having greatest difficulties, as indicated by the high score in the key area.

Understanding the key areas

Engagement

A child who is engaged will play – exploring and experiencing the world through all their senses. This engagement assists a child's cognitive development and enables them to become more competent. A child who is engaged will extend and adapt an activity. They will show eager anticipation of activities and will participate spontaneously. They will remain motivated, focussing on the activities available rather than being aimlessly distracted by what is around them.

Where engagement is lacking there is cause for concern about the child emotionally. Lack of engagement can be a sign of disaffection when a classroom activity (part of the curriculum) seems meaningless, frustrating and boring. Engagement occurs when activities are enjoyable and familiar – or sufficiently novel that the level of challenge is not too difficult but not too easy. Engagement is not the same as stereotypic, repetitive activity which indicates anxiety and may be tied to the child's need to organise (or systemise) information (Baron-Cohen, 2009). Stereotypical activity is different from disengagement, where the child shows no interest in activities other classmates are engaged with and may demonstrate learned helplessness.

Lack of engagement can arise from several attachment issues. It can mean that the child does not feel safe enough to explore – even a familiar toy or activity. Withdrawing from positive engagement is one of the two strategies insecure children have to reduce their anxiety. Some children learn that the best thing to do when feeling unsafe is to shut down or withdraw emotionally. This may happen if the child has learnt that they are "on their own" when they are emotionally upset. The child will become emotionally bereft and hide their emotions. This will occur when they believe that adults will not support them and that the best way to reduce stress is to become emotionally detached. This emotional detachment spreads over into a detachment from playing and engaging in an activity.

Relationships

When children experience consistency and warmth through secure relationships with adults, they gain a sense of security. They develop the confidence to explore the world and create relationships with others throughout their whole life. These relationships start in infancy with the adults' reactions to the sounds, cries, facial expressions and actions of a baby. The adults' responses and their attunement to these signals teach the child how to relate to others. Babies and young children experience attunement ("tuning in or having the ability to be at one with another") when they know that an adult recognises their signals (crying, holding arms out or vocalisations) and understands their needs.

Attentive, responsive and loving care sets the foundation for a child's capacity to form close relationships. A child with secure attachment will seek out adults for positive interactions. They learn to be accessible, responsive and approachable by others. They are happy to receive attention – to receive a hug, a smile, a gentle touch, a compliment, a word of comfort or encouragement.

Some children have particular issues with relationships – for example developing a sense of empathy is extremely difficult for some children. This is particularly true for children with ASD – who are often described as having difficulties with a theory of mind (Baron-Cohen, 2009). Empathy can be seen when children learn to understand that their feelings are important and that other people have feelings too which may be different to their own. Even developmentally young children can show concern for a crying peer or may cry themselves in "attunement" with their friend.

Without these secure relationships there is no one to contain the child's emotional distress. As a result, they don't learn to regulate their own emotions and, once aroused, find it very difficult to calm down or regulate themselves. One of the two most common ways for a child to deal with the overwhelming nature of this is to intensify the emotional demands they place on those around them. The child's internal working model tells them that they must magnify or intensify their emotional demands in order to receive emotional support.

In addition, some children with disabilities are hypersensitive to particularly sensory stimuli – sound or lights. They may become over stimulated and need to look down or away, avoid you, squirm to get away, turn in a different direction or become disruptive. Once aroused they may be unable to calm and regulate themselves. This response to sensory stimuli may be misunderstood as a challenging emotional outburst rather than a response to being overwhelmed by the sensory stimuli.

When a child has not experienced containment of their overwhelming feelings through secure early relationships, they will form their own response patterns. They learn to respond in a variety of ways and will repeat the patterns that have had the most impact in reducing the overwhelming nature of the level of emotional arousal. The most successful in some situations may be emotional withdrawal, and in others it may be to intensify the response in order to obtain more attention from the supporting adults. Over time the most "successful" patterns will be at the core of how a child forms, or avoids, relationships with others. Whichever pattern the child uses adults will find these logical, but inappropriate, emotional reactions stressful and difficult to relate to – thus perpetuating the child's relationship difficulties.

Feeling positive

There is a cognitive component as well as an emotional component to well-being. The cognitive component is expressed in thinking positively. This is based on feeling safe but is an extension of it. Concepts such as resilience, self-esteem and having fun take precedence.

When children feel positive about themselves, their environment and those around them they are happy and at ease. They take pleasure in what they are doing and interacting with others. They are open and receptive to learning. Feeling positive significantly impacts upon their capacity to be receptive to new and potentially challenging changes in their environment. When they do not feel positive, they are more resistant to change

Understanding emotional difficulties

and may attempt to control their environment in order to reduce the anxiety. They may lock themselves into self-soothing or self-stimulating activities or self-injury.

The Fishbone (Diagram 3.1.1) identifies several well-researched factors that impact on how the child with learning difficulties and complex needs feels safe and positive. These included the experience of early separation from carers, family security, interaction and learning difficulties. These factors may cumulatively impact on the child's self-esteem. A child who experiences being valued, loved and accepted for who they are, experiences high self-esteem. They engage with others with the expectation that they will be liked, and that people will want to spend time with them. Feeling positive is also tied to feeling that you have some control over your world. If you are not involved in any decisions – even something as routine as what you eat for lunch – you may not feel that you have much autonomy. When a child has high self-esteem, or self-confidence, they are willing to embrace new activities or experiences. If their confidence is low, they can be more rigid in their behaviour and fearful or reluctant to try anything new or different.

Resilience is fundamental to children's emotional growth and stability, it is the capacity to recover quickly from difficulties or changes. Children build resilience through supportive relationships that enable them to overcome challenge and cope with change. A child with severe or complex learning difficulties requires adults to plan on their behalf, to begin to build that resilience early in life in order to maximise their potential for independence and autonomy as they grow.

The issues highlighted by the Individual Profile can also be drawn on a Fishbone with Engagement, Relationships and Feeling Positive as the three spines. An example of this is given in Example 3.2.1 for Musa. Notice how there are several issues in each area. Each issue highlights a potential focus for change.

Complete the Fishbone using information from the Individual Profile on a child whose emotional well-being is of concern

Supporting an individual child

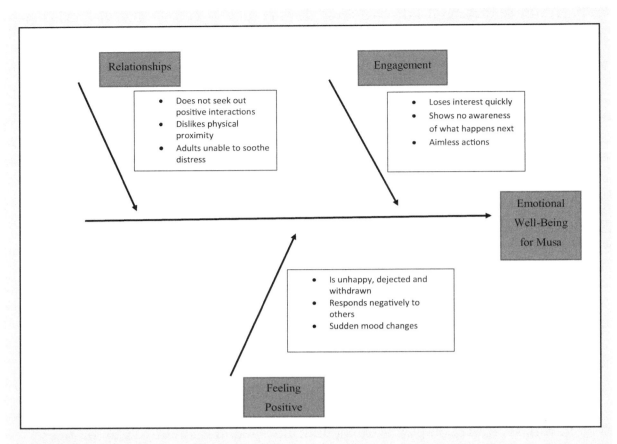

Example 3.2.1 Musa – Fishbone of Individual Issues

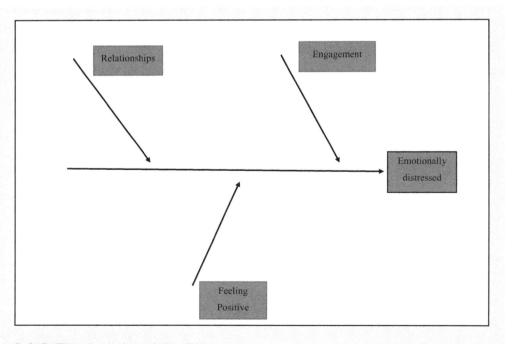

Activity 3.2.2 The Individual Profile

Developing class-based solutions using Solution Circles

The previous two chapters have explored how many children with severe and complex learning difficulties are also more exposed and vulnerable to having emotional difficulties. Ways of identifying the difficulties they have in terms of Engagement, Relationships and Feeling Positive have been provided. In this chapter, the focus is on what the class team can do to alleviate these emotional difficulties using a technique called Solution Circles (O'Brien, Forest, & Pearpoint, 1996).

Individual children's emotional well-being can be supported in several ways. The child can be supported with internal, environmental and interactional changes:

Internal: the focus here is on changing and improving a child's responses to their environment without deliberately altering the latter. This might include developing communication skills or building self-esteem and resilience. This can be achieved using therapeutic techniques such as psychotherapy, or play, drama or music therapy.

Environmental: the focus here is on changing and enhancing the environment around the child. This might include increasing family security and reducing stress by advocating for better access to facilities in the community, including housing and play facilities in the school holidays. This may include working in partnerships with community and advocacy projects.

Interactional: the focus here is on building positive relationships so that the child develops secure attachments and the ability to emotionally regulate themselves. This includes providing opportunities for engaging with adults and peers through structured and unstructured interactions. Communication is the key to this, the way you initiate and respond to any and all forms of communication by the child.

The focus of Emotionally Able is on the interactional factors in the school but the importance of the other areas should not be overlooked especially when community-based solutions are being considered. At this stage however the focus is on what you as a class team can do to support the child. There is however one other relationship that has a direct bearing on the class team's work – that is your involvement with the parents. Before using a Solution Circle to decide on a strategy, you need to meet the parents to discuss how they see the situation.

Meeting with parents/carers

Before developing a school-based plan for supporting a child, it is important to meet the parents. The class teacher, or the EWB coordinator, should call this meeting. It can be a brief meeting – 10 to 15 minutes – but it is best done face to face, rather than by an email or phone call. This is not a problem-solving meeting but rather one that ensures that the parents' viewpoint is known and they are aware of your concerns. This meeting has two purposes:

To give information:

- *Why you are concerned?*
- *The issues you are particularly concerned about – i.e. share the completed Fishbone*
- *What you are intending to do – i.e. hold a Solution Circle meeting*

To receive information:

- *Are there similar issues at home?*
- *When does this happen/not happen?*
- *What changes, if any, have there been at home?*

If the child seems much more emotionally settled at home than they are at school, it is well worth revisiting the classroom strategies to try to help the child to settle. Vice versa if the child is very emotionally unsettled at home as well as at school then having the parents involved is vitally important.

Working assumptions

With the information from the Individual Profile and the discussion with the parents, you can begin to develop possible working assumptions to help develop an understanding of the child's emotional difficulties. The working assumptions, or hypotheses, are tentatively held explanations that can be used to guide further questioning and information gathering that will form the basis of an agreed plan. The essential purpose of working assumptions is to help all those involved to understand the child's emotional difficulties and why particular interventions may be successful. The working assumptions should do the following:

- Summarise the child's main difficulties.
- Show how the child's difficulties affect one another.
- Incorporate a developmental and psychological understanding – such as attachment theory – which helps make sense of the child's difficulties.

- Give rise to a plan of intervention.
- Are open to be reviewed and reformulated over time.

(see Johnstone & Dallos, 2014, p. 11)

The working assumptions (see Diagram and Example 3.3.1) can be seen as developing ideas or "hunches" that are possible explanations about what is presently going on based on the understanding of all those who are supporting the child. This can incorporate developmental and psychological theories but should always firmly reflect what is known about the child and the information gathered. They are shared (tentatively) with other members of the class team at the next stage, to help develop a plan of how to move forward.

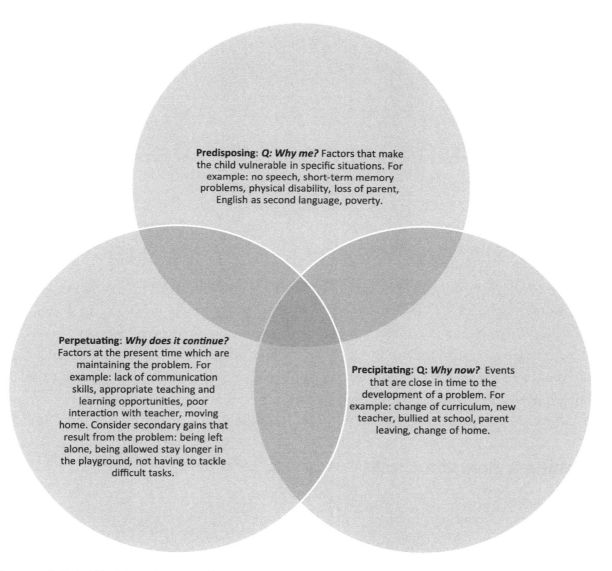

DIAGRAM 3.3.1 Working Assumptions

Supporting an individual child

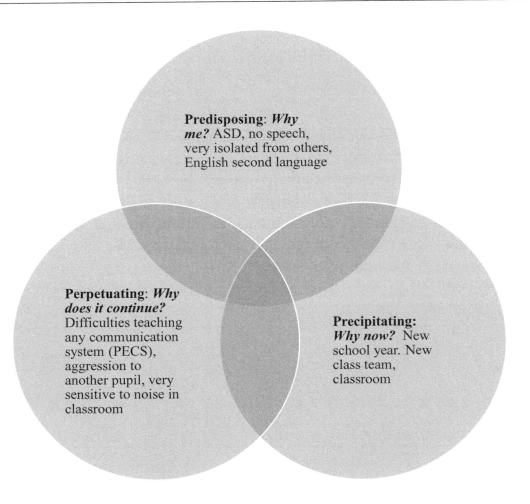

EXAMPLE 3.3.1 Musa – Working Assumptions

Solution circle

We have found Solution Circles a very useful process for enabling the class team to decide on a strategy. Solution Circles were initially developed to support inclusion (O'Brien, Forest, & Pearpoint, 1996). Their aim is to help staff discuss school issues as a group, and to generate solutions. Solution Circles are a very positive way of helping the class team develop solutions to support the emotional well-being of children with severe and complex needs. Each circle takes no more than thirty minutes and involves the class team who listen, discuss and collaborate around the emotional well-being of an individual child.

Running a Solution Circle

The roles:

Presenter of the problem – Class teacher

Facilitator and time keeper – EWC coordinator

Developing class-based solutions

> Note taker or graphic recorder
>
> Brainstorm team – the classroom team
>
> Observers – parents/carers

The EWB coordinator needs to explain/remind everyone of their role and the steps to be followed. It is important to ensure that parents/carers are included in the process, but they understand that their role is simply to be observers. The focus of the Solution Circle is on the class team taking responsibility for the child's emotional well-being in school. There should be no expectation that parents will change what they are doing. There is the opportunity for them to do this at the next stage.

Step 1 (6 minutes)

The class teacher takes 6 uninterrupted minutes to outline the problem. They should present information from the Individual Profile and meeting with parents and include the working assumptions about the predisposing, precipitating and perpetuating factors. The EWB coordinator keeps time and makes sure that no one interrupts. The recorder takes notes or draws a picture. Everyone (the classroom team) listens. If the class teacher stops talking before the 6 minutes elapse, everyone else stays silent until the 6 minutes pass. This is vital! The problem presenter gets 6 uninterrupted minutes.

Step 2 (6 minutes)

This is a brainstorm. Everyone chimes in with ideas and creative solutions to what they have just heard. It is not a time to clarify the problem or to ask questions. It is not a time to give speeches, lectures or advice. The facilitator must make sure this is a brainstorm. Everyone gets a chance to give their brilliant ideas. No one must be allowed to dominate. The problem presenter listens – without interrupting. They must not talk or respond. The note taker keeps a record.

Step 3 (6 minutes)

The group now have a conversation led by the class teacher. This is time to explore and clarify the problem. Rate where the problem is now on a scale from 0–10. Focus on the positive points – only what can be done in the classroom, or school, not what cannot be done. Focus on what would improve the problem by one point on the scale.

Step 4 (6 minutes)

The class teacher and the class team decide on first actions that are do-able within the next 3 days. At least ONE action should be initiated within 24 hours. This is critical.

Unless the first action is taken almost immediately, people do not get out of their rut. The EWB coordinator confirms that they will see the person within 24 hours and check that the first action has been implemented. They also need to set a review date when they will check with the class team if there has been any change in the child's emotional well-being. This should happen in the next 2 or 3 weeks.

Finally, the group just does a round of words to describe the experience and the recorder gives the record to the class teacher.

For further information about Solution Circles visit their website – www.inclusion.com.

Comments

- A Solution Circle will not resolve the mental health issues of a child with a disability (or any other child). However, what it will help with is getting the team "unstuck". By using the rating scale, the team can see that it is not about reducing the emotional difficulties to zero – instead it is about reducing the difficulties by 1 point. By doing this, the class team can feel that they have some power over the emotional difficulties.
- The class team need to be realistic about the time frame they are working in. Step 4 in Solution Circles requires the first action to be initiated within 24 hours. This is what the class team will do. However, the child will not change overnight – in fact they may not react to this change for a few days or even weeks.
- If, within a few weeks, the class team can see that there are some small changes in the child's emotional well-being in terms of engagement, relationships and feeling positive, then the Solution Circle can be repeated. New actions can be decided upon and acted on by the class team.
- However, if there appear to be no changes then the team can move to Stage 3 which involves a more complex process of the involvement of the wider community.

Core active ingredients

There are many different strategies or interventions the class team can use to support the emotional well-being of children. Whatever first step is decided upon there are common core active ingredients across different types of intervention. The following three ingredients are the core of any strategy:

> **Relationship:** the most important factor is the "working alliance", the relationships both between members of the class team and with other stakeholders, e.g. the parents. They must all feel that you are working together for the emotional good of the child.

Aims: tied to this is the agreement on the aims of the intervention and the first steps to achieve change. If members of the class team have different views on the purpose of the plan, let alone the ways of going about it, then change is unlikely to occur.

Meaning: the third most important factor is a change in people's understanding of the child's emotional problems – a transformation of meaning. At the end of the Solution Circle there should a fundamental shift in how people see the emotional issues of the child. This may be around a better understanding of why they are so emotionally distressed, but it also may be a feeling of empowerment by the participants as they finally see a way forward.

Solution Circle provides a process that allows the class team to put in place a plan to support the emotional well-being of a distressed child. Once the process becomes familiar to the class team it is relatively easy to find 30 minutes to convene the Solution Circle again to review the plan and to think of the next actions. The strength of a Solution Circle is that it allows the class team to take some control of the situation rather than looking to outside agencies to understand what is happening in the classroom. There is however a place and time for outside agencies involvement, and this is dealt with in the next chapter.

3.4 Developing community-based solutions using the multiagency team and quality circles

Working with the wider community

Emotionally Able focusses on how school staff can support a child's emotional well-being in school. However, a child's mental health and emotional distress will also be seen in their home and when they are out in their community. There are several reasons why it is important for the school, and in particular the EWB coordinator, to work with the wider community:

1. From a parent's point of view, their child cannot be divided into segments of how they are at school or at home. The child's emotional difficulties may be more evident in different situations, but they will be there. In fact, it can be argued that if the child is only emotionally distressed in one situation, for example at home, or at school, then they do not have mental health difficulties but are simply reacting to a stressful environment that needs to be changed or altered.

2. However, recognising the differences in the child's emotional well-being in these diverse situations can help identify ways of alleviating emotional distress. For example, many of the Classroom Strategies (from Section 2) can be adapted and used by parents in the home.

3. Within the wider community there are a range of experienced professional in teams involved with the mental health of children. These services include Children and Adolescent Mental Health teams (CAMHS), Children with Disabilities Teams (Social Care), the Educational Psychology Service and many school's Multidisciplinary Teams (MDTs), which include physiotherapists, occupational therapists and speech and language therapists. They can do the following:

   - Help to shift and widen perspectives, sharpen the focus and overcome blind spots.
   - Provide different resources on how to support the child's emotional well-being.
   - Ensure that all three types of factors – individual, environmental and interactional are addressed.

Mental health difficulties are usually of a long-standing and all-pervasive nature. Solution Circles will begin to give you some influence over a child's emotional well-being in school. However, to further extend that influence you may need to involve other agencies – individuals and teams outside the school including, of course, the child's parents and carers. Part of the role of the EWB coordinator is to establish links with the other agencies. These links will range from informal – for example telephone and digital communication where information is shared – through to more formally representing the school at meetings called and chaired by other agencies.

Sometimes the EWB coordinator will need to call a multi-agency meeting to support the work being done with a child in school. In these circumstances, using techniques adapted from both Solution Focussed approaches (Lloyd & Dallos, 2006) and Quality Circles (Robson, 1982), provide a structured approach that recognises the roles of all participants and values their understanding and insight.

What is a Quality Circle?

The essential idea of a Quality Circle (QC) is a group of people, who do the same or similar work, meeting together to identify, analyse and solve problems in their work and, where possible, implement solutions. Quality Circles were developed in Japan as a way of stimulating their economy. Their effectiveness means that they are now used all around the world in businesses as a way of making improvements in the workplace. Quality Circles should not be confused with Quality Circle Time which is a different, innovative way of working with children and young people (Mosley, 2005).

Quality Circles (QCs) are a helpful way of bringing together participants from the various agencies who know the child and have a role in supporting them. The model that we use differs from a traditional QC in a few ways. In businesses the focus of QCs is, naturally enough, on improving the quality of the goods being manufactured, or the service being provided. The focus for Emotionally Able is solely on improving the emotional well-being of a child. In addition, we use Solution Focussed techniques to enhance these meetings – many of these techniques have already been introduced in Emotionally Able. Over the years several valuable lessons have been learnt that make QCs successful as a way of organising meetings.

Participants know the child: participants need to know the child. These QC meetings work best when everyone present knows the child – parents, school staff, physiotherapist, psychologist, social worker, etc. These are not "talking shops" but practical meetings – the aim is to come up with actions that the participants at the meeting will implement. It may be helpful to have a limited number of people present who do not know the child – but they often cannot really contribute to the discussion at the required level.

Participants take ownership of the problem and the solutions: QCs reinforce the fundamental idea that the people who know the child best are also the people who know how to resolve the problem. It is the people who work with the child daily – the class team, the parents, the lunchtime assistants – who hold the keys to helping the child develop and change. Sometimes they will need support from people in the wider community of professionals for ideas and support but essentially it is what happens on a day-to-day basis that makes a difference to the child's emotional well-being.

Participants select problems: QCs work on the problems that the participants select. These are not imposed by anyone – the Head Teacher, parents, psychologists or someone outside the circle. This is crucial. This selection may be initiated by the class teachers briefing the QC on what they have already done, but it may then be changed or modified by the other participants. In this way it ensures that the people who know the child best are all working towards the same end.

Working as a team: there are no hierarchies in QCs. The EWB coordinator's role is to support the process not to dominate the discussion. You need to ensure that all participants have a say, that their voices are heard and that they are involved in the decision making. The fact that different participants will have different views about ways forward should be a strength of the circle. However, this is not a talking shop – the focus is on what the participants are going to do at the end of the QC meeting.

The gold in the mine: this refers to the fact that when people who know the child, and are asked in the right way, they will have the knowledge and understanding of the child to affect their emotional well-being. The gold in the mine is the expertise and experience of the people who know the child. This means that solutions are already available to people if they only knew where to look and how to start to mine them.

No quick fix: a key principle of all QCs is that there are no quick fixes. If a problem was easy to solve, it would have been sorted out a long time ago. Emotional difficulties are, by definition, longstanding and it will take time to change the Internal Working Model in an emotionally distraught child. For children with severe and complex learning difficulties, all learning takes time and patience. The aim is to ensure that short-term improvements will have a long-term impact on the quality of their lives as adults.

Setting up the Quality Circle

The EWB coordinator needs to take responsibility for setting up and running the Quality Circle. Central to the success of the QC is the involvement of the parents or carers. Ensuring that they can attend is the first step. In the same way that children become anxious when they do not know what to expect, it is helpful to put clearly in writing what the purpose of the QC meeting is and how it will be organised. In particular, the length and structure of the meeting can be clarified. This information is also important when introducing the Quality Circle for the first time to professionals in other agencies.

> Dear Ms Bene
>
> Thank you for confirming that you can attend the Quality Circle meeting on the 7th February from 2:00–3:30. The focus of the meeting will be on developing Musa's emotional well-being. As you know Ms Jean has been working with the class team on a number of strategies and we want to discuss how the progress they have made can be extended.
>
> At the meeting we will discuss:
> - What is happening now – Ms Jean will tell the meeting about what the class team are presently doing
> - What would be helpful to Musa
> - What we can all do to help support Musa's emotional well-being
>
> I think it will be a very helpful meeting as everyone there knows Musa and they and you will have a chance to share their knowledge and skills.
>
> Best wishes
>
> Angela Davis (Emotional Well-Being Coordinator)

Example 3.4.1 Musa – Letter of Confirmation

Structuring the quality circle meeting

There are three stages to the Quality Circle meeting:

- The present situation
- The preferred situation
- Strategies

The EWB coordinator's role is to chair the meeting and to manage the process by introducing some of the techniques that are described in the following sections. Not all these techniques will be used in all meetings and you, as the EWB coordinator, will need to use your experience to judge when it is helpful to introduce a particular technique. It helps everyone's focus if they keep in mind that the last stage requires an agreement by participants to act! Many of the techniques are visual and it is helpful to have a white board or flip chart and a colleague to help with drawing and writing. It is your role to encourage people to talk and to remain focussed – not to judge what is going on. People will not contribute if they are feeling they are being judged. The group should be working from the premise that "if what we are doing now is not working what can we do differently". It may be helpful at the end of each stage to summarise what has been said as a basis for moving forward.

Stage 1: The present situation

Aims:

- To ensure that everyone feels that they have an active role in the Quality Circle
- To ensure that everyone is listened to
- To understand how different situations affect the child emotionally
- To shift and widen perspectives on the child
- To hear about participants' present involvement

Following a confirmation of the aims, organisation and timing of the meeting, participants should be invited to introduce themselves.

The class teacher should then briefly explain the work that has already been carried out through the Solution Circle. Participants should then have the opportunity to briefly describe how they find the child and the emotional issues that the class teacher has described. The aim is to develop a shared understanding about the child's emotional well-being in terms of Engagement, Relationships and Feeling Positive.

Additional techniques

Post-its:

Aim – To ensure that everyone feels they have an active role and are listened to

Give everyone a post-it. Ask them to write on the post-it the emotional issue that they are most concerned about. Draw three circles on the flip chart (Engagement, Relationships and Feeling Positive). Ask each participant to say in which circle their post it should be placed. Do not disagree with their choice of circle – they may be seeing things in a different way to you. However, allow people to move their own post-it to a different circle as the discussion unfolds.

The child's perspective

Aim – To shift and widen perspectives

This technique has already been introduced in Section 3.1. The aim is to try to see things from the child's point of view. This is about trying to place yourself in their shoes, and thinking if they could talk what would their explanations of the emotional distress be. The benefit of having different adults at the meeting is that they will have different ideas about what the child is feeling and would say. The more varied the group the more likely that new ideas of insights will follow from this activity.

Developing community-based solutions

> Think of the child whose emotional well-being is causing you concern. If they could say why they became so upset and distressed what would they say?
>
> They would say:

ACTIVITY 3.4.1 What Would they Say?

The Fishbone

Aim – To develop a picture of all the factors that are affecting the child's emotional well-being This technique has been introduced in Section 3.2. The aim is to put into one picture the issues that the child has. The simplest Fishbone has three spines with the three areas of Relationships, Engagement and Feeling Positive represented. By completing this, the QC meeting can capture the child's emotional difficulties in these different areas.

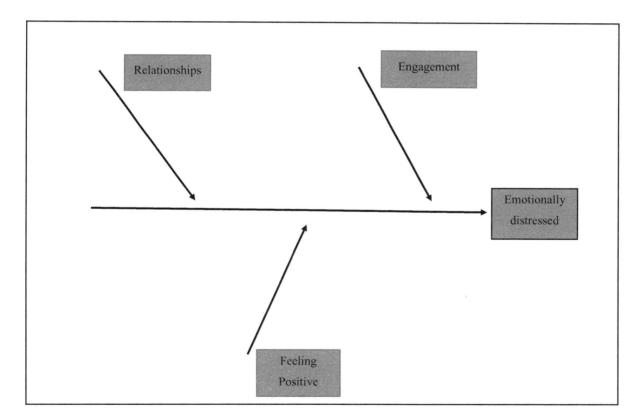

ACTIVITY 3.4.2 A Fishbone of Factors

Stage 2: The preferred situation

Aims:

- To explore new possibilities and perspectives
- To understand what is blocking changes in what people do
- To decide on an area to focus on
- To explore possible aims
- To set a specific aim for what participants want to achieve

The second stage is about focussing on what you are trying to achieve in terms of the child's emotional well-being. The Quality Circle needs to agree on an aim for the support for the child's emotional well-being. This should narrow the focus to one area: Engagement, Relationships or Feeling Positive based on the discussion at Stage 1. Some of these issues will have been identified by the class teacher from the Individual Profile; however, the discussion is likely to have widened and deepened the understanding of the issues. Having settled on an area, the QC should decide on what the aim of the action will be. It is helpful to focus the aim on how you want the child to be emotionally – rather on what you don't want them to be. In that way the focus is on the left-hand side of the constructs on the Individual Profile. This aim can be made more specific using the Scaling technique (see Example 3.4.2).

Musa: Issues identified by the Individual Child Profile and confirmed at Stage 1 of the Quality Circle:

Engagement:
- Loses interest quickly
- Shows no awareness of what happens next
- Aimless actions

Relationships:
- Does not seek out positive interactions
- Dislikes physical proximity
- Adults unable to soothe distress

Feeling Positive:
- Is unhappy dejected and withdrawn
- Responds negatively to others
- Sudden mood changes

Following discussion, the QC meeting decided that Relationships was the most important area and in particular: "Adults unable to soothe distress".

Agreed Aim: Emotional Distress is Soothed by Adults

EXAMPLE 3.4.2 Musa – Focussing on an Area and Issue

Additional techniques

Miracle Question:

Aim – To shift focus to the child's perspective

The miracle question is the starting point for helping the QC decide on its aim and in developing well-formed goals for the child (see Lloyd & Dallos, 2006). It gives participants in the QC permission to think about what the child would be like if they did not have emotional difficulties.

> Miracle question:
> *"I want you to imagine a time in the future when a miracle has happened and that Musa no longer had a difficulty with Relationships – what would have changed?"*
> - He would play with the other children.
> - He would not get so upset and try to hit people.
> - **He would calm down quicker. ***
> - He would seek out support from trusted adults.
> - He would be willing to accept change from trusted adults.

EXAMPLE 3.4.3 Musa – Miracle Question

In this example the QC identifies several things that would have changed but decided that the most important miracle that would have happened is they think that *we could get him to calm down quicker.*

Scaling

Aim – To narrow and clarify the aim

Scaling helps to clarify and decide on the aim. The technique is also from Solution Focussed Therapy. Scaling is a series of questions that helps to narrow and focus the aim so that it is more manageable. In this way you are turning the aim into a goal. Start by rating on a scale from 1–10 where the child is now.

> Scaling:
> OK, so if 10 is Musa distressed and out of control all the time and 1 is completely calm, where would we put him on the scale – OK 8?
> **Then ask what it would look like if he moved down one point on the scale.**
> OK, so he is an 8 now what would it look like if he moved one point down the scale to a 7?
> OK, so what we are saying is he would be a 7 if we could get him to calm down quicker once he is distressed.
> **You can then ask what would need to be different to help him to calm down quicker.**
> OK, so what might we do to get him to calm down quicker? What do we need to do?

EXAMPLE 3.4.4 Musa – Scaling

These scaling question implicitly acknowledge that the QC recognises that emotional difficulties are often deeply ingrained and difficult to change. By recognising the small difference that can be made, it helps participants feel that they can make a difference and remain motivated. This leads naturally into the next stage of developing strategies.

Exceptions questions

Aim – To help see opportunities for change

This is an especially helpful technique during QC meetings as participants will have seen the child in different situations. Exceptions are those occasions when the problem is less severe or does not occur at all. Exceptions focus on the conditions – the time and situations which seem to affect the problem.

> Exceptions:
> OK, in the last few weeks who has seen Musa calm down quickly when he was distressed?
> OK, so we have several examples including just before lunch in school when he was brought into the corridor and once at home when you sat opposite him on the sofa and had a cup of tea. Any others?
> So, what do you think was different about that day?

EXAMPLE 3.4.5 Musa – Exceptions Questions

By drawing attention to the exceptions, participants will be reminded that the child does not have these emotional difficulties all the time.

Stage 3: Strategies

Aims

- To focus on ways of achieving the aim
- To develop strategies that can be used at home, in school and in the community
- To obtain commitment to action
- To confirm a way of reviewing their success

By this stage the QC should have a good idea about the emotional issues of the child and how different situations affect them. There should be agreement about the most important area to tackle and some of the exceptional circumstances when it is less of a problem. They also will have a view on the specific aim – how to move the child one point down on the scale. All this information can be captured on an Action Plan.

Developing community-based solutions

\multicolumn{6}{c}{ACTION PLAN – EMOTIONAL WELL-BEING}

		Name of Child: Musa			
Date	Area	Aim	Present Rating	Preferred Rating	Specific Aim
10th Feb.	Relationships	Emotional distress is soothed by adults	8	7	He would calm down more quickly

Strategies	By Whom?	Start date
We would keep calm and talk to him	All	14th Feb.
Speak softly	Mum	11th Feb
Sing nursery rhyme	School Staff and Mum	14th Feb,

Review Date: 3rd April

EXAMPLE 3.4.6 Musa – Developing an Action Plan

Once the specific aim has been decided on the QC needs to identify what can be done to make this change happen – to move the child down one point on the scale.

Q. So, what can we do differently? What actions are we going to take?

This can take the form of a discussion. However, the additional technique, the "How/How", described next, is also an extremely effective way of helping the QC generate strategies for moving forward.

Additional techniques

How/How:

Aim: To generate practical actions that address the specific aim

The How/How provides a visual summary of the ideas that the QC has come up with for making the change actually happen. The specific aim is put into the box on the far left, in our example, the aim is "He would calm down quicker". The QC is then simply asked "How (could this be achieved)"? A range of strategies are agreed and then recorded in the next column of boxes. Arrows are then used to link from the

Supporting an individual child

original statement box to the first column of potential new strategies. For each of the new potential strategies "How" is asked again. As new strategies are generated, they form a new column to the right and have arrows linking then to the previous strategy. As new columns are generated a pathway can be seen from the original statement through to the final potential actions that will begin to be implemented by the QC. Some of the thinking about the importance of Boundaries, Holding and Containment may enter the discussion. And in fact, some of the strategies for action may initially be stimulated by ideas from the Classroom Strategies (see Section 2). However, the How/How should not be limited by these but come from the QC discussion about the present and preferred scenario.

The power of the How/How is that, as you move from left to right, the actions get simpler and more manageable and concrete. This means that you can keep generating ideas until participants reach a level that they can begin to implement. Once the different lines of strategies are generated, the QC needs to decide on which strategy or strategies they will use. It is often helpful to start with only one or two.

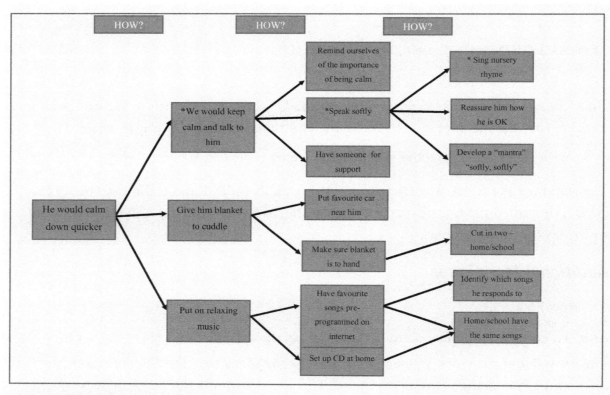

EXAMPLE 3.4.7 Musa – How/How

The How/How helps the QC feel empowered. Often one of the reasons for calling the QC meeting is that participants feel stuck – not certain how to help the child. By generating a range of strategies collaboratively to support the child's emotional well-being, the QC participants feel empowered and have some control over the situation.

Sometimes it is helpful to switch the focus of the How/How to ensure all participants feel that they are involved in the process. In this case the first level could become school, home and community. This allows the QC participants to think more directly about what they are going to do in their situation.

The How/How ensures a range of strategies are created to help the child's emotional well-being. In the example for Musa three initial "first level" strategies are identified – practical things that people can do. The question "how" was then asked again and seven second-level strategies were identified which then led to the final six strategies. This is simply an example for Musa. The QC can move to four- or five-level strategies if you want to and there is no limit to the number of strategies that can be generated for each level. It should also be noted that sometimes a strategy may run out at a particular level while others continue.

The idea is to generate as many strategies as possible using the experience of the QC participants to generate new ideas. At the end of the process the QC can decide on which of the pathways they think will be most successful. In this example it was decided that "We would keep calm and talk to him – ensuring we all spoke softly – and whispered a familiar nursery rhyme to him". The group then went on to discuss what was the best nursery rhyme for him. The agreed Actions from the How/How are entered on the Action Plan. (For Musa these are * on the How/How).

		ACTION PLAN – EMOTIONAL WELL-BEING			
		Name of Child: Musa			
Date	*Area*	*Aim*	*Present Rating*	*Preferred Rating*	*Specific Aim*
10th Feb.	*Relationships*	*Emotional distress is soothed by adults*	*8*	*7*	*He would calm down more quickly*

EXAMPLE 3.4.8 Musa – Completing an Action Plan

Supporting an individual child

The How/How focusses the QC participants on what they can do. Completing the Action Plan ensures accountability. The Action Plan includes a review date. There are different sorts of review dates.

- One review date – like the Solution Circles – is to check that the person has started doing what they said they would.
- Another review date is to check how things are going.

One of the most helpful things the EWB coordinator can do is to follow up the agreed actions. Usually this will be informally face to face with the class teacher or parent, or by phone. QCs are time intensive and in certain circumstance you may follow up with another meeting though it is more likely that this will be done informally. It is important not to judge people if they haven't been able to complete their actions, but rather to see this as helpful information about the problems the child is having.

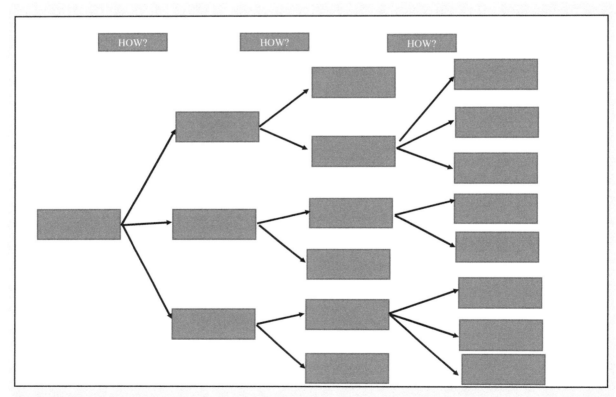

Activity 3.4.3 A How/How for a Child's Emotional Well-Being

ACTION PLAN – EMOTIONAL WELL-BEING					
Name of Child:					
Date	Area	Aim	Present Rating	Preferred Rating	Specific Aim

Strategies

ACTIVITY 3.4.4 An Action Plan

Obtaining a commitment to action

It is at the final stage when deciding on what strategies to use that participants recognise just how instrumental they are in supporting the emotional well-being of the child. To make a change in the emotional well-being of the child, they will have to adjust or adapt something that they are presently doing. While it is the child who has the emotional difficulties, it is the adults around who are going to have to change how they engage and relate to the child.

Participants may sometimes try to avoid acting by suggesting that it is other people's responsibility to do something. So, the class team may think that the Head Teacher needs to reduce the number of children in their class, or the parents may think the class teacher needs to be firmer, or the social worker may feel this is a housing problem.

These changes and the introduction of new strategies may sometimes make participants feel vulnerable. However, what often happens is that the process has the opposite effect. Small steps and a supportive, no-blame atmosphere will help build participants confidence. Participants leave the QC meeting feeling that their concerns have been listened to, that some practical actions have been decided, and that they are involved in helping the child. They also know that there is a team of people around the child – all of whom are committed to supporting their emotional well-being. Adults need this support – as well as the child.

Supporting an individual child

At all times the EWB coordinator needs to be warm and supportive – keeping the conversation on solutions not problems with a forward-looking agenda. Part of the conversation may be around who else could support or help the participants but the focus all the time at this stage is what the participants in the QC can do. This is why participants in QC should already be actively involved with the child. This is a group who are going to act on the problem – not just talk about it.

At the end of the QC the EWB coordinator should summarise the process and thank all the participants for their involvement. This helps all participants see what has been covered through this process and the progress that has been made in developing ways to support the child's emotional well-being.

Postscript – it takes a village to raise a child

Everyone who reads this book will have a narrative or a story about working with children with emotional difficulties. Everyone creates a narrative about their teaching – about children they have worked with and classes they have taught. These stories may be clear and coherent or at times fragmented and disconnected. These stories are not only individually constructed but co-constructed with the other people in your classroom, your school and your personal life. These stories help make sense not only of the successes you have had dealing with children with emotional difficulties – but also when you had problems. Over your career these stories about dealing with emotional well-being will change as you deal with new children and old incidents are given new meaning.

In Emotionally Able we have tried to put together a narrative that will help you support the emotional well-being and mental health of children with severe and complex learning difficulties. This narrative has come from our own experiences and those of the teachers and parents that we have worked with over the years. From these experiences we have constructed in Emotionally Able two interlinked narratives. One of these narratives is about why children with severe and complex learning difficulties have emotional difficulties. The second narrative is about what every member of the school staff can do to support these difficulties.

During our working lives we have heard many different narratives about children with severe and complex learning disabilities also having emotional difficulties. In fact, for many years their emotional needs were not even acknowledged but left out of the discourse. This was the time when behavioural psychology was the dominant narrative and the focus was only on what could be observed – rather than what was experienced and internalised by the child. The study of what went on inside the child's head was not seen as scientific. By closely observing (and counting) the incidences of unwanted (challenging) behaviour using ABC charts, and noting, and then changing, the contingencies (antecedents and consequences), the narrative was that the child's behaviour, and emotional outbursts, would change. Emotional outbursts were seen as challenging behaviour due to a history of inappropriate reinforcement.

The next narrative that we experienced in our work was one where the child's behaviour problems were a skills deficit. Their frustration and anger were due to their limited skills. The solution was curriculum based and the need to teach new skills. At

Postscript

the same time in mainstream schools the introduction of the National Curriculum was seen as the mechanism to raise standards. This narrative was gradually refined into a deficit model around the child's inability to communicate and to express their views. The solution once again was skill based – to teach communication skills – and this led to the use of many communication systems including Signing, Objects of Reference, and PECs (Picture Exchange Communication).

In our work we have touched on other narratives around emotional well-being and mental health too. These include narratives from other professionals, for example medication, and other cultures – for some, the role of religion and punishment for previous sins. The common thread among all these narratives are people's need to create a story that makes sense of their experiences – and a way to take some control of negative or problematic experiences. It is through narratives that we try to make order and control in a confusing and uncontrollable world.

So, the title of our narrative around Emotionally Able is that *It takes a village to raise a child.* This simple saying captures much of the story of Emotionally Able. It applies to how the material was developed, how EWB coordinators should see their role, as well as how a child with emotional or mental health difficulties can be supported.

Emotionally Able takes a whole school approach. Originally, we had been asked by a special school to address the issue of which children should receive specialist therapy from inside and outside the school. It gradually became apparent that this issue was the tip of an emotional iceberg. So, we started by addressing how we understand and assess the children's needs within the school. From here, we noted that, to do this, we needed to see how the whole school understands emotional well-being before prioritising the development of emotionally supportive classrooms. This was done by working with the whole school – believing that change is more likely to happen if the whole village is involved in deciding what to do. Workshops where staff's experiences of the emotional aspects of their work were explored and recorded were then developed into the Classroom Strategies. Based on an interlinked narrative around the emotional issues of individual children, we devised a way of identifying the issues that individual children were having through the Individual Profile of Emotional Well-Being. By ensuring there were forums where all staff members could share their views, we were able to hear both the dominant and the more marginalised narratives of experienced staff. We ensured that the whole village was involved in these discussions.

Over time, this material as presented here has undergone numerous revisions and transitions where we have organised and re-structured the material to give it a strong narrative about how it can be most effectively used by EWB coordinators and school staff. To these experiences we also added developmental and psychological perspective

Postscript

which we felt helped make sense of these experiences. We see these as views from our wider "professional" village. To achieve this there was a "flip/flop" of ideas between our experiences and the different theoretical perspectives. We visited and revisited a range of theoretical perspectives from established dominant ones such as behavioural psychology and Piagetian development through to more radical ones like Daniel Kahneman's "Thinking, Fast and Slow". Gradually it became clear that the most important development and theoretical perspectives that helped give a clear narrative were John Bowlby's attachment theory and Ferre Laevers' work on well-being. Gradually these ideas became more coherent and are now presented here as part of Emotionally Able.

In the same way, we think that EWB coordinators, or Mental Health Leads, need to work with the whole school team to develop an emotionally supportive environment in their schools. The structure and activities contained in this book is a starting point that will need to be adapted to the particular circumstances of the school. In this way we see EWB coordinators being the most successful when they use the whole village (in this case the school) to raise the child. The EWB coordinator needs not only the help from the village elders (the SLT) but also the whole village – including the other children – recognising that everyone has a role to play. Often emotional problems arise at lunchtime or staff breaks and staff who maybe come in for only a few hours a day have a key role in supporting emotional well-being. The EWB coordinator needs to feel that they can rely on the whole village to support their difficult – and emotionally demanding work. They need to feel safe – as well as the child.

Finally, of course we have stressed throughout the book that everyone involved with the children need to work together. The Classroom Strategies only work if the whole class team agrees to implement change. Some rely on one person taking the lead, but most require a shared responsibility to implement. In particular we have stressed the sense of security that the child needs to feel that can only be achieved if the world, and adults' reactions and interactions with them are calm, consistent and predictable. If the child feels unsafe in one situation this will spill over into others as well. So, it is really the whole village, the whole school, that needs to develop a culture of calm support.

We are aware there are parts of the village that we have not touched on in this book. In particular, the central importance of the parents and the whole family. This is not because they are not important. On the contrary they are so important that only another book would really do their involvement justice.

One of the things we have stressed in Emotionally Able is the importance of focussing on the future and using the Classroom Strategies and Solution and Quality Circles to make things better. All too often the discourse around emotional well-being and mental health is negative and is problem saturated. This can become a problem:

Postscript

> A discourse of deficits provides continuing escalating difficulties, whereas a discourse of competence, strength and resilience promotes the amplification of those very qualities.
>
> (Wagner & Watkins, 2005, p. 6)

We are aware that we all construct and create the problems or concerns we present. Equally we construct and create the solutions.

In Emotionally Able we have tried to outline a coherent story about how to support children with severe and complex learning difficulties and additional emotional difficulties. We have offered activities and ideas that are coherent and themed. We have established a path along which a class team or a whole school can travel with a beginning, (developing a shared understanding), a middle (introducing Classroom Strategies) and an end (supporting, and getting others to support, the individual child). This is a linear process so that the story is clear, however, we are aware this is an artificial progression and each EWB coordinator and class teacher will need to find their own path in their own context. We have tried to provide a sense of agency in Emotionally Able by organising the sequence of activities to provide a positive momentum moving forward.

The purpose of Emotionally Able is not to give all the answers to all the difficulties for all children with emotional problems. It is helpful to see the EWB coordinator more like a landscape gardener for the village. Your job is not about pruning trees and cutting grass. Instead it is about helping others take up new positions in their garden so that things can be seen in a different light. Your job is to help staff take up a more empowered position where their experiences, sensitivity and skills are used as the bedrock of making a difference to the emotional well-being of children.

So, we will finish with 10 final points about using the whole village to raise the child:

1. Whatever view you have now, whatever the dominant narrative is on emotional well-being in your school, the important first step is recognising that others, teachers, LSAs and parents may have different views.

2. Meanings are jointly created through conversations – if there are no conversations between the staff there is no shared understanding.

3. Take an experiential and reflective approach about what is valuable and positive about the experiences and stories they have constructed.

4. Polarisation can occur in schools when staff are ascribed divergent meanings and identities (the SLT, the LSAs, the playground supervisors). This can escalate to where people do not communicate with each other.

5 Staff can become problem saturated by the narratives and culture around them.

6 Emotionally Able allows you to co-construct ways of helping children with emotional difficulties.

7 Emotionally Able allows you to create a positive, empowering discourse about how to support children.

8 The EWB coordinator needs to be mindful of the power in the title and recognise that using it may disempower others.

9 You need to recognise that over time your ways of helping children with emotional difficulties will change.

10 Our framework for using Emotionally Able cannot be yours – but can be the starting point for you to create your own narrative for helping your school to support the emotional well-being and mental health of children with severe and complex learning difficulties.

References

Baron-Cohen, S. (2009). Autism: The empathizing – systemizing (E-S) theory. *Annals of the New York Academy of Sciences*, 1156, pp. 68–80.

Bowlby, J. (1969). *Attachment and loss, Vol. 1: Attachment*. New York, NY: Basic Books.

Bowlby, J. (1988). *A secure base: Parent-child attachment and healthy human development*. New York, NY: Basic Books.

Brown, R. (2018). *Mental health and wellbeing provision in schools: Review of published policies and information*. Research Report 837. London: Department for Education.

Department of Education. (2012). *Training materials for teachers of learners with severe, profound and complex learning difficulties*. Available at: www.complexneeds.org.uk. (Accessed 5 April 2019).

Department for Education. (2015). *Mental health and behaviour in schools: Departmental advice for school staff*. London: Department for Education.

Department for Education. (2018). *Mental health and behaviour in schools: Departmental advice for school staff*. London: Department for Education.

Department of Health. (2015). *Future in mind: Promoting, protecting and improving our children and young people's mental health and wellbeing*. London: Department of Health.

Department of Health and Department for Education. (2017). *Transforming children and young people's mental health provision: A Green paper*. London: Department of Health.

Emerson, E. and Hatton, C. (2007). The mental health of children and adolescents with learning disabilities in Britain. *The British Journal of Psychiatry*, 191, pp. 493–499.

Every Disabled Child Matters. (2007). *Disabled children and child poverty*. London: National Children's Bureau.

Frederickson, N., Dunsmuir, S. and Baxter, J. (2009). Introduction. *In*: N. Frederickson and S. Dunsmuir, eds. *Measures of children's mental health & psychological wellbeing: A portfolio for education & health professionals*. London: GL Assessment.

Gardner, W., Graeber-Whalen, J. and Ford, D. (2001). Behaviour therapies. *In*: A. Dosen and K. Day, eds. *Treating mental illness and behaviour disorders in children and adults with mental retardation*. Washington, DC: American Psychiatric Press, pp. 69–100.

Gutman, L. and Vorhaus, J. (2012). *The impact of pupil behaviour and wellbeing on educational outcomes*. Research Report 253. London: Department for Education.

Hamblin, E. (2016). *Gender and children and young people's emotional and mental health: Manifestations and responses*. London: National Children's Bureau.

Her Majesty's Government. (2004). *Children Act 2004*. London: Her Majesty's Stationery Office. Available at: www.legislation.gov.uk/ukpga/2004/31. (Accessed 4 April 2019).

House of Commons Education and Health Committees. (2017). *Children and young people's mental health: The role of education*. First Joint Report of Session 2016–17, HC 849, para. 43.

Howe, D. (2006). Disabled children, parent: Child interaction and attachment. *Child and Family Social Work*, 11:2, pp. 95–106. doi.org/10.1111/j.1365–2206.2006.00397.

References

Johnstone, L. and Dallos, R. (2014). *Formulation in psychology and psychotherapy*. 2nd ed. East Sussex: Routledge.

Kitchener, B., Jorm, A. and Kelly, C. (2010). *Mental health first aid manual*. Melbourne: University of Melbourne, ORYGEN Youth Health Resource Centre.

Laevers, F. (Ed.). (2005). *Well-being and involvement in care settings: A process-oriented self-evaluation instrument (SiCs)*. Brussels: Kind & Gezin.

Laevers, F. (2011). Experiential education: Making care and education more effective through well-being and involvement. *In*: R. Tremblay, M. Boivin, and R. Peters, eds. *Encyclopaedia on early childhood development*. Available at: www.child-encyclopedia.com/child-care-early-childhood-education-and-care/according-experts/experiential-education-making-care. (Accessed 8 November 2018).

Lloyd, H. and Dallos, R. (2006). Solution-focused Brief Therapy with Families who have a child with intellectual disabilities. *Clinical and Child Psychology and Psychiatry*, 11:3, pp. 367–386.

Moran, H. (2010). Clinical observations of the differences between children on the autism spectrum and those with attachment problems: The Coventry Grid. *Good Autism Practice*, 11:2, pp. 46–59.

Mosley, J. (2005). *Quality circle time in the primary classroom: Your essential guide to enhancing self-esteem, self-discipline and positive relationships*. Trowbridge: Positive Press.

The National Association of Independent Schools and Non-maintained Special Schools (NASS). (2007). *Making sense of mental health*. Available at: www.nasschools.org.uk. (Accessed 4 April 2019).

National Autistic Society. (2010). *You need to know*. Report 914. Available at: www.nas.org.uk. (Accessed 4 April 2019).

National Health Service (NHS). (2018). *Mental health of children and young people in England (2017)*. NHS Digital. Available at: https://digital.nhs.uk/data-and-information/publications/statistical/mental-health-of-children-and-young-people-in-england. (Accessed 4 April 2019).

National Institute of Health and Care Excellence (NICE). (2008). *Social and emotional wellbeing in primary education*. Manchester: National Institute for Health and Care Excellence.

National Institute of Health and Care Excellence (NICE). (2009). *Social and emotional wellbeing in secondary education*. Manchester: National Institute for Health and Care Excellence.

National Institute of Health and Care Excellence Guidelines (NICE). (2015). *Challenging behaviour and learning disabilities: Prevention and interventions for people with learning disabilities whose behaviour challenges*. Manchester: National Institute for Health and Care Excellence.

O'Brien J., Forest, M. and Pearpoint, J. (1996). *Solution circles*. Toronto: Inclusion Press. Available at: www.inclusion.com. (Accessed 4 April 2019).

Pappas, R. and Frize, M. (2010). *Intellectual disability mental health first aid manual*. 2nd ed. Adapted from B. Kitchener, A. Jorm and C. Kelly, *Mental health first aid manual*. Melbourne: University of Melbourne, ORYGEN Youth Health Resource Centre.

Parkin, E. and Long, R. (2018). *Children and young people's mental health: Policy, services, funding and education*. House of Commons Briefing Paper 07196. London: HMSO.

Public Health England. (2015). *Promoting children and young people's emotional health and wellbeing: A whole school and college approach*. Available at: www.gov.uk/government/publications/promoting-children-and-youngpeoples-emotional-health-and-wellbeing. (Accessed 4 April 2019).

Robson, M. (1982). *Quality circles: A practical guide*. Brookfield, VT: Gower Press.

Seligman, M. and Darling, R. (2009). *Ordinary families, special children: A systems approach to childhood disability*. 3rd ed. New York, NY: Guilford Press.

References

Stirling, S. and Emery, H. (2016). *A whole school framework for emotional wellbeing and mental health: A self assessment and improvement tool for school leaders.* London: National Children's Bureau.

Wagner, P. and Watkins, C. (2005). Narrative work in schools. *In*: A. Vetere and E. Dowling, eds. *Narrative therapies with children and families: A practitioners' guide to concepts and approaches.* London: Routledge.

Weare, K. (2015). *What works in promoting social and emotional well-being and responding to mental health problems in schools? Advice for schools and framework document.* London: National Children's Bureau.

Wells, J., Barlow, J. and Stewart-Brown, S. (2003). A systematic review of universal approaches to mental health promotion in schools. *Health Education*, 103:4, pp. 197–220.

Whiting, M. (2014). Children with disability and complex health needs: The impact on family life. *Nursing Children and Young People*, 26:3, pp. 26–30. Available at: https://journals.rcni.com/doi//pdf/10.7748/ncyp2014.26.3.26.e388. (Accessed 4 April 2019).

World Health Organization (WHO). (2014). *A state of wellbeing.* Geneva: World Health Organization. Available at: www.who.int/features/factfiles/mental_health/en. (Accessed 4 April 2019).

Index

Note: Page numbers in **bold** indicate a table and page numbers in *italics* indicate a figure on the corresponding page.

Action Plans 102, 103, 107–108
altruism 46
Antecedents, Behaviour and Consequences (ABC) charts 109
anxiety 4, 13, 19, 20; insecure children's reaction to 72–73; *see also* common strategies to reduce anxiety
Attachment theory 65, 68, 72, 76, 111; attunement 83; early separation 65, 66; insecure attachment 68–69; internal working model (IWM) 70, 71, 72, 84, 96; and resilience 85; secure attachment 5, 45, 65, 68–69, 71
attention difficulties 20
auditing 32–33; reflective audit 32, 33, 34
autism spectrum disorder (ASD) 3, 18, 20, 77

boundaries 73–74
Bowlby, John 65, 70, 111

challenging behaviour 3–4, 18, 21, 22
Children and Adolescent Mental Health teams (CAMHS) 94
classroom strategies 34, 44, *44*, 111; engagement 45; feeling positive 50–51; relationships 45–46, 50
class teams 40, 63, 73; altruism 46; auditing the present situation 32, 33; emotional well-being of 13; emotionally supportive classrooms, developing 31; formal and informal role of 13–14; organisation sub-categories **49–50**; prevention of mental health problems 29; supportive 46
cognitive information 70
committing to action 107–108

common strategies to reduce anxiety: containing 75–76, 84; holding 74–75, 104; setting boundaries 73–74
community-based solutions 87, 94
containment 75–76, 84, 104
Coventry Grid 77

Department for Education (DfE) 8; advice for school staff 17; on developmental disorders 20; list of mental health problems 19–20; on prevention of mental health problems 29
Department of Health (DH), *Transforming children and young people's mental health provision* (2017) 6
developing relationships 45–46

educational attainment, and emotional well-being 16–17; National Curriculum 110
Education, Health and Care (EHC) plan 16–17, 22
emotional distress 4; and emotional outbursts 64, 109; and mental health problems 18; self-regulation 71, 84
Emotionally Able 4, 6, 14, 16, 20, 24, 29, 35, 40, 87, 94, 95, 110, 111, 112, 113; "classroom strategies" 32, 34; engagement 4–5; implementing 14; Road Map Planner 8–11; strategies for change 34, 35; teamwork 12–13; Vision Statement 24–26; whole school approach to emotional well-being 7–8
emotionally supportive classrooms, developing 29, 30, 31; auditing the present situation 32, 33; collating the evaluations 40–41; evaluation 38; implementing strategies for change 34, 35; repeating the cycle 40; when to start 30

Index

emotional problems: anxiety 19; depression 19, 20

emotional well-being 15, 16, 23, 31, 63, 112–113; factors affecting 23, 24, *24*; formal and informal role of the class team 13–14; internal support 87; policy and research on 24; whole school approach 6, 7, 24

Emotional Well-being (EWB) coordinators 3, 8, 29, 40, 41, 92, 110, 111, 112; obtaining a commitment to action 107–108; Quality Circles (QCs) 96; role of in Solution Circles 91; setting up Quality Circles (QCs) 96–97; team leaders 14; teamwork 12–13; working with the wider community 94–95

empathy 83–84

Engagement 17, 29, 32, 38, 44, 45, 77, 82, 87, 100

environmental support 87

evaluation 39–41

Evaluation Records 38, 40; collating 40–41

family security 67, 68

feeling loved 46; altruism 46; family love 46; sub-categories of *58*

Feeling Positive 5, 16, 29, 32, 44, 77, 84–85, 87, 100

feeling safe 46; sub-categories of *56*

Fishbone diagram 65, *66*, 70, *72*, 85, *86*, 99

friendship 13, 46

Future in Mind report 7

gender, effect on reactions to distress 73

holding 74–75, 104

hypersensitivity to stimuli 84

identifying triggers of emotional outbursts 64, 65

Individual Profile of Emotional Well-Being 77–79, 80–81, 88, 110; engagement 82–83; feeling positive 84–85; and interpretation 83–84; relationships 83–84

insecure attachment 68–69

insecurity, feelings of: and family security/relationships 67, 68; reacting to anxiety 72–73; and separation from caregivers 65, 66

intensifying emotional reactions 72, 73

interactional support 87

internal support 87

internal working model (IWM) 70, 71, 72, 84, 96

involving the family 88

Laevers, Ferre 4, 30, 111; experiential approach of 4–5

Leuven Involvement Scale 4

mental health problems: anxiety 19; and conduct disorders 21; defining 17–19; defining World Health Organization (WHO) 16; depression 19; developmental nature of 24; diagnostic overshadowing 20; incidence 18, 22, *22*, 24; labeling 18–19; prevention 29

miracle question 101

multidisciplinary team (MDT), working with the wider community 94–95

Musa 63, 64, 65

National Autistic Society 20

National Children's Bureau, advice for children's emotional well-being 15

NICE Guidelines 21, 22

Office for Standards in Education, Children's Services and Skills (Ofsted) 17

policy and research: on the emotional well-being of children with severe learning disabilities 15; on supporting emotional well-being of children 24

Quality Circles (QCs) 95; Action Plans 102, 103; the child's perspective 98; exceptions questions 102; the Fishbone 65, *66*, 70, *72*, 85, *86*, 99; How/How 103–104, *105*, *106*; miracle question 101; obtaining a commitment to action 107–108; outlining the preferred situation 100; outlining the present situation 98; participants 95–96; post-its 98; Scaling technique 101, *102*; setting up 96–97; strategies 102, *103*; structuring 97

Relationships 5, 29, 32, 44, 45–46, 77, 87, 92, 100; developing 45–46; family 67, 68;
resilience 15, 84, 85
Road Map Planner 8–11

Scaling technique 100, 101, 102
school leadership team (SLT) 6, 8, 40; emotional well-being of 13; working in a team 12–13; *see also* class teams
school staff: containing a child's distress 75–76; emotional well-being of 13; obtaining a commitment to action 107–108; roles of in Solution Circles 90–91; teamwork 12–13; working with the wider community 94; *see also* class teams
secure attachment 5, 45, 65, 68–69, 71
self-esteem 84, 85
self-regulation 71, 84
self-soothing 71
separation from caregivers 65, 66
severe and complex learning disabilities 3, 65; cost of raising children with 67, 68; diagnostic overshadowing 20; incidence of mental health problems in children with 22, 22, 24; interactional difficulties of children with 68–69; and the internal working model (IWM) 70, 71, 72, 84, 96; and mental health problems 21, 23; Musa 63, 64, 65; treating as a skills deficit 109–110; *see also* common strategies to reduce anxiety
shared communication systems 45; sub-categories of 52
social, emotional and mental health (SEMH) needs 3, 16–17, 23; supporting children with 3

Solution Circles 87; aims of the intervention 93; brainstorming 91; core active ingredients 92–93; deciding on do-able actions 91–92; group conversation 91; meeting with parents 88; outlining the problem 91; rating scale 92; roles in 90–91; time frames 92; understanding the emotional issues of the child 93; working with the wider community 94–95
Solution Focussed Therapy 101; exceptions questions 102; miracle question 101
special education needs (SEN) 16, 20
Standard Attainment Tests (SATs) 16
stereotypical activity 83
strategies for change 44, *44*; engagement 45; implementing 34, 35; relationships 45–46; "thinking big" 34, 35, 40
strengths of a whole school approach 7–8
structure of the day, sub-categories 48

teaching: planning for a whole school approach to emotional well-being 7; strategies for change 45

United Kingdom (UK): educational achievement 17; National Curriculum 110

Vision Statement 24–26

whole school approach to emotional well-being 6, 7, 30, 40, 110; arguments for 7–8; planning for 7; Road Map Planner 8–11; Vision Statement 24–26
withdrawing emotionally 72, 83
working assumptions 88–89

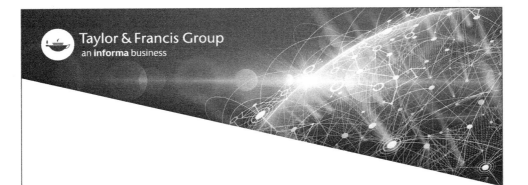

Taylor & Francis eBooks

www.taylorfrancis.com

A single destination for eBooks from Taylor & Francis with increased functionality and an improved user experience to meet the needs of our customers.

90,000+ eBooks of award-winning academic content in Humanities, Social Science, Science, Technology, Engineering, and Medical written by a global network of editors and authors.

TAYLOR & FRANCIS EBOOKS OFFERS:

- A streamlined experience for our library customers
- A single point of discovery for all of our eBook content
- Improved search and discovery of content at both book and chapter level

REQUEST A FREE TRIAL
support@taylorfrancis.com